# BEYOND RESISTANCE

# BEYOND RESISTANCE

## COPING WITH THE STRESS OF THE TRUMP ERA

*An Essential Guide*

KATHY HERTZ & DONNA LIPMAN

BLISS
PUBLISHERS

This is a Bliss Publishers book
Copyright © 2018 by Kathy Hertz and Donna Lipman

Throughout this book, we have used stories and examples designed to help the reader better understand the concepts and process. The stories are composites and some names have been changed to protect identities and to ensure confidentiality.

All rights reserved. No part of this publication may be reproduced, distributed, or transmitted in any form or by any means, including photocopying, recording, or other electronic or mechanical methods, without the prior written permission of the authors, except in the case of quotations permitted by copyright law.
For permission requests, contact the authors via email: *info@beyondresistancebook.com*.
For more information, visit *www.beyondresistancebook.com*.

Published in the United States of America
First Printing 2018

ISBN: 9780692106105 (hardcover)
ISBN: 9780692105450 (paperback)
ISBN: 9780692105467 (epub)

Cover design by Suzette Vaughn
Cover photograph: Bryan Woolston, Women's March on Washington 2017.
Interior design and graphics: Duane Stapp
Printed in the United States

To all those who have stood up for peace and human rights, inspiring countless others to do the same.

▼

For my husband, Tom Parish. You are my life's greatest delight. Every day I am blessed with the song you have awakened in my heart. I love you more.

—Donna

▼

For my son, Sam Kinter. You make me want to be a better person every day. I love you more than my heart can hold.

For my father, Richard Hertz. You have taught me compassion, generosity, and to stand up for my beliefs. You have always encouraged me to fly toward my dreams. I love you.

—Kathy

*The ultimate test of a man is not where he stands
in moments of comfort and moments of convenience,
but where he stands in moments of
challenge and moments of controversy.*
—Martin Luther King, Jr.

# Table of Contents

Preface ................................................................. 1
Beyond Resistance ............................................... 3
Mirror, Mirror, on the Wall ................................. 19
I Just Can't Take It Anymore! ............................. 29
I Gotta Be Honest ............................................... 47
Self-Care as a Revolutionary Act ........................ 59
Ready, Set, Go! .................................................... 77
The Fatal Four .................................................... 107
From Finger-Pointing to Freedom .................... 129
Can We Tawk? ..................................................... 137
Epilogue .............................................................. 149
Endnotes ............................................................. 153
Additional Resources ......................................... 159
Acknowledgments .............................................. 165
About the Authors .............................................. 169

# Preface

Dear Reader,

If you didn't vote for Donald Trump on November 8, 2016, you probably woke up to the news of his victory with feelings of shock and despair. The unexpected outcome of the election was surreal, unlike anything we could have imagined or believed possible. It was a nightmare come true. It was enough to send any non-Trump voter over the proverbial edge. If you voted for Trump and regret that decision, you may also feel some of the same distress. Trump's election has left us in uncharted waters, and many of us are drowning in our stress. We are enraged, frustrated, and frightened, believing that the President of the United States is nothing less than an existential threat.

It is our desire as life coaches to support you during this time and provide tools and strategies to help you manage your emotions while listening to the day's news, conversing with a Trump supporter, or simply thinking about the state of our union. It is our wish that you use your time effectively to resist in a way that works for you, understand and handle your overwhelming stress, and maintain the energy and desire to stay engaged. And through the process of learning to better cope, you will notice yourself transformed into a greater version of yourself. You will notice qualities and talents that you may not have previously known existed within you. We hear again and again the stories of people who are proud of who they are becoming *because* of Trump—more vocal, informed, courageous, engaged, and empowered. It is our intention that reading this book and doing the exercises lead you to a sense of awe as you witness your transformation.

Whether you are a political observer, advocate, or activist, whether you create or share an occasional Facebook post, send postcards to elected officials, or organize a march, you play a vital role in influencing the direction we move in as a nation. It is imperative that we each stay engaged, believe in ourselves, use all our skills, and support one another.

*Beyond Resistance* will guide you on your resistance journey. We will help you clarify who you want to be, what you want to do, and how you want to do it. You will experience shifts in perspective that will ripple throughout your life.

And we will be right there with you, every step of the way.

With love and gratitude,
Donna and Kathy


P.S. We want to hear about your journey—both your successes and your challenges. Please share with us and the rest of the *Beyond Resistance* community on Facebook (*http://www.facebook.com/BeyondResistance*), Twitter (*@BeyondResistanc*), or by email (*info@beyondresistancebook.com*).

INTRODUCTION

# Beyond Resistance

Most of us thought it was a joke when we heard Trump was running for President. How could anyone take this guy seriously? This was the reality television host who insisted that President Obama was not born in this country. Surely it was only a matter of time before one of the more experienced, qualified, and serious Republican candidates emerged as the party's nominee.

Well, as we all know, that didn't happen. Bill Clinton was called the Comeback Kid and Ronald Reagan the Teflon President—but what Trump pulled off was beyond description. We watched a surreal campaign and were disturbed when Trump gained as much traction as he did. What seemed like a multitude of reasons he should be sent to political purgatory only added to the zeal of his fans and disciples. We were concerned and confused that people didn't see what we saw—or even worse, saw the lies, juvenile behavior, racism, misogyny, and bullying, but didn't care. We began to feel separate from "those" people and couldn't believe that our country could fall for such divisive and seemingly hateful—even violent—tactics. We were troubled by what was happening but held onto the belief that it would all be okay once Americans went to their polling places and did the "right" thing.

*It wasn't.*

We were not prepared. We curled up in bed and cried, eventually emerging in a state of shock and sadness, walking around like zombies. What happened? What do we do? We imagined that this was what a military coup might be like. We felt powerless and defeated and didn't know how to move forward. Since Vietnam, we could not recall a time when our country had been so divided. The election caused us to question who we were as a nation. Was this still our country? Did we still belong?

The *Beyond Resistance* story began with the election of Trump, but our personal story unfolded five years ago when we were serendipitously brought together as teacher and student. Donna, originally from Los Angeles but living in Austin, Texas, is a singer and presentation skills instructor with The University of Texas. At the time of our meeting, she was also a program leader for The Ford Institute, a center for emotional and spiritual education created by best-selling author Debbie Ford, an internationally acclaimed expert on the shadow and personal transformation. Debbie passed away in 2013 but created a legacy of ten books, nearly one thousand coaches, and the life-transforming Shadow Process workshop. Donna was scheduled to lead the institute's coach training program in the fall of 2012.

Kathy, originally from Manhattan, relocated to Washington, DC, as part of the Clinton presidential transition team in 1992. She served as a political appointee at the White House and Pentagon through most of Clinton's eight-year administration. In 2012, Kathy was

## Introduction

raising her son and seeking her next career path when a friend gave her a copy of Debbie Ford's *The Dark Side of the Light Chasers*. She found the book so compelling and powerful that she signed up for the three-day Shadow Process workshop, and subsequently, for the Fall 2012 coach training program. During the first class meeting, Donna introduced herself as the course leader and when her turn came, Kathy introduced herself as one of the students. Throughout the next eighteen months of the course, we got to know each other, and upon its completion, a lasting friendship blossomed. We spoke almost monthly, simply catching up on our lives, until Trump was elected. Then everything changed...

We must admit that as transformational life coaches, we both pride ourselves on the work we do with others and fully trust that we have the skills and tools to navigate any bump in the road we might face. We are experts in guiding clients beyond their internal resistance to enable them to act, achieve their goals, and enjoy a newfound sense of freedom in their lives. We are highly skilled at supporting clients in breaking through barriers that block them from achieving their dreams. Our tools had served both our clients and us well, and we were secure in the knowledge that the teachings and practices we subscribe to—choosing faith over fear, embracing all of who we are, practicing forgiveness, and understanding the enormous role our stories and limiting beliefs play in who we believe ourselves to be and what we achieve—would help us weather any storm.

But we were thrown into a tailspin by the knowledge that Trump, who had run a campaign of division and hate, would be president of our United States. We were unable to find a way to accept this and began to question our work and some of the core principles to which we ascribe: that surrendering to *what is* is key to empowered action, that we are a reflection of the world around us, and that we are responsible for our thoughts and actions. We had met our match in Trump and were depressed, afraid, and stumped. One thing was certain: no one was coming to save us. We needed to figure it out. We wanted to understand how we could apply all that we knew to this situation, which seemed to fall outside the realm of anything we had previously experienced.

You may be in a similar place, realizing that your go-to tools to relieve stress and cope simply aren't cutting it. Maybe you practice yoga or meditate, but these activities are no longer enough; perhaps you usually connect with friends and talk things through when you are overwhelmed, but that isn't working either. Most of us have come to terms with the fact that dealing with this new reality is is definitely going to take more than a glass of wine or some deep breathing!

By the end of January 2017, we were both in very dark places. We couldn't shake a sense of doom. How could this have happened? Who are these people who believe Trump is their savior? How can we live in the country that elected this man? These were pressing questions that we didn't have answers for, and they were impacting us and our lives. We and most of our friends, family members, clients, and colleagues were living with an underlying anxiety, and we noticed that it was beginning to affect us negatively. We had shorter fuses and less joy. We had trouble sleeping. Many of us had a constant knot in our stomachs. We needed to figure out how to lift ourselves up out of victimhood and powerlessness into empowered action and strength. At this point, the two of us decided to have weekly calls and support each other in coping with this new reality. We were determined to use the chaos as a catalyst for growth rather than be swallowed up by it.

## A Resistance Is Born

In December 2016, we began to hear a buzz about a women's march that would take place in Washington, DC, on January 21, 2017, one day after the inauguration. The buzz grew louder, and before long there were hundreds of thousands of people expected to descend on the National Mall from all over the country, with additional rallies being held around the world. Millions who couldn't attend a rally planned to show their support by watching these events on television. On January 21, 2017, the resistance was born. It was as though someone said, "You've had your cry; now get into action," and millions responded by showing up peacefully yet strong and resolved. One could not be anything but inspired seeing over a million (mostly) women come together to take a stand and knowing many more were behind them remotely.

At the Women's March, most of us realized we had a collective voice that could not be ignored or silenced and we each would play an important role in holding Trump and his administration accountable. Staying informed and taking action would be essential. We understood that we would not be millions if each one of us did not make the decision to stand up and be counted. The Women's March highlighted that we are all connected—not just here in this country, but with others around the world who share our values. It also demonstrated how much we all *yearn* to be connected and how empowering it is. On that day, we experienced a unifying vision of compassion and equality that propelled us forward.

Following the Women's March, many of us stepped into committed action. Whether as participant or observer, watching the birth of the resistance was exhilarating. People threw themselves into this new revolution and became intensely responsive to day-to-day events, showing up at rallies and town halls, making calls, and sending postcards. Many believed they had to do it all because if they didn't, the outcome would be dire. And what do you do when you are facing consequences this severe? Everything you can. We tried to stay informed and dove in heart and soul, determined to save the world. We played full out, gave it our all, didn't hold back. We made more calls, sent out more postcards, and showed up for more marches and protests.

We were running in one hundred different directions at once, trying to stay on top of it all, but beginning to feel as if we couldn't keep up. Perhaps making the effort to stay informed was all we could handle, or we were acting but convinced we weren't doing enough, being enough. Many of us didn't take the time to take stock because it all seemed so incredibly important.

And then the deluge of headlines began:

"Roe v. Wade Hanging in the Balance"

"EPA Website Dismantled—Climate Change Removed from White House Website"

"Muslim Ban"

"24 Million to Lose Health Care"

*Introduction*

"Deregulation—Dumping in Our Rivers and Streams"

"Endangered Species List Endangered"

"Animal Abuse Hotline Shut Down"

"DACA Protections Hanging in the Balance"

"Mandatory Minimum Sentencing"

"ICE Raids"

"Alternative Facts"

The list went on. Every day there was something new and unthinkable.

How could we possibly stay calm or slow down in a climate like that? We kept going, believing that our lives and the world depended on it. We told ourselves stories about how awful "those" people were; we experienced firestorms of anger inside us and used them to propel the engine of our revolution. We each created different realities, stories about what it all meant, and we held different fears. We believed that our country was making a sharp U-turn back from the progress achieved during the Obama administration. We saw an attempt to reverse women's, minorities', and LGBTQI rights. We witnessed racism and intolerance become acceptable, the lines of separation between church and state grow blurred, and big business interests take priority over our environment. We learned that millions would lose health care and that a crazy person now had his finger on the nuclear button. It was the perfect storm and overwhelm was inevitable.

Articles began to appear in the national news and medical journals, such as the *American Journal of Psychiatry*, citing a jump in

Americans' anxiety levels. On the one hand people were having serious discussions about checking out of politics or moving to Canada. On the other hand, it was evident that the resistance had grown in size and momentum and its members had become more confident. It is clear that the resistance is here to stay as long as Trump remains in power.

It is essential that the time remaining in Trump's presidency (and we must remain committed to action so that he will not achieve a second term) be treated as a relay, not a marathon, and that we pace ourselves if we are going to make it to the finish line. Long-term overwhelm is not an option. We must take time to stop and evaluate. But is it possible to stay on top of it all or believe that we are ever doing enough? Can we mitigate the stress and upset? Can we stay engaged and resist, or even follow the news, without falling apart? The answer is yes, and you will find solutions to these and other questions in this book.

Writing *Beyond Resistance* has been a learning process and an indispensable part of our personal journeys to find well-being and balance since the election. It has helped us recognize that this era of socio-political turmoil is also a time of wonderful opportunity for us to access parts of ourselves and nurture qualities that we may have been unaware of or denied in the past. Have you recognized that you are a strong organizer or leader or that you are able to speak publicly with clarity and courage? Are there other parts of yourself you are noticing for the first time? Have you realized that you are creative, organized, committed, confident, outspoken, passionate, adventurous, engaged, persuasive, well-spoken, socially conscious, perceptive, smart, rebellious, or curious? Trump is inadvertently providing endless opportunities for us to grow!

## It Is What It Is

After the election and inauguration, one of the first and most difficult coaching concepts that we both had to re-embrace is how critical it is to acknowledge and accept what is. No, we are not talking about accepting the fact that there is nothing you can do so you may as well be quiet and suck it up. We don't mean you shouldn't work to make a difference or that things can't change. We are all about change-making, but it is important to recognize that digging your heels in, becoming entrenched in what you believe *should be*, and refusing to acknowledge what *is*, leads to stagnation. It is a form of denial. And when you are in denial, it's virtually impossible to move forward because you are unwilling to accept the facts of a given situation. How can you create change if you don't view circumstances clearly as they are?

It is a natural human reaction to deny and resist those things that feel wrong or dangerous. It is normal to want to throw a hand up and yell an emphatic NO! to what we experience as threatening. And while resistance can be a motivator, coupled with denial it inhibits and holds us back from creating what we desire most. Initially, we spent an exorbitant amount of time and emotional energy refusing to accept the facts of our political reality. This is pretty ironic because as life coaches, we consider ourselves resistance busters! But rather than use our time and energy to create solutions and effect change, we were bogged down in our refusal to move beyond what we thought should be; we were stuck in the mire of hate and disgust for Trump, his supporters, and his administration and its policies. We spent hours on the phone together, beginning each call with "WTF??!!" Endlessly complaining and working ourselves up, we made ourselves sick, experiencing stomach upset, insomnia, and anxiety. Yes, this motivated us to take action, but we were exhausted from the negativity of wrestling with reality. It was only after we came to terms with the facts that we were able to step into more powerful, committed action. With newfound clarity, we looked around us and feared that if we and other resistance members like us did not slow down, accept what is, and take stock of the direction in which we were headed, we would soon face a public health crisis. We recognized the importance of focusing our energy on what we stand for rather than what we are fighting against.

Once you are willing to acknowledge a situation or circumstance exactly as it is, you are able to make conscious choices as to how you will proceed. Trump is President. You can refuse to accept this fact all day long, but it is still a fact. If you spend a tremendous amount of internal energy refusing to accept it, insisting that "I cannot deal with the fact that he is president" or "I refuse to accept that he is president," you will be hindered in your ability to step into powerful activism. This holds true not only in your resistance but in all other areas of your life.

Outrage and the refusal to accept what is have created a powerful resistance movement that has reminded us what we love about our nation—the courage, compassion, commitment, innovativeness, and leadership of its citizens. But as evidenced by our own experience, resistance without insight limits our effectiveness. The difficulty arises when you waste precious energy "resisting" reality instead of using your resources toward achieving your goals. Resisting reality immobilizes you as you dig your heels into the sand and try desperately to keep the pain and fear of what is from washing over you. Rejecting the fact that Trump is president is a perfect example. To reiterate, we are not talking about agreeing with what is but accepting that it is at this moment. This realization removes the power that it holds over you and releases you from the chains of fighting reality. You are then free to decide how to proceed to effect the change you want to see. Dwelling on negative, dark, and heavy thoughts and worries obscures solutions and choices that might otherwise present themselves. Acceptance allows us to act from a fresh, unencumbered place and opens up new and exciting possibilities.

Actor Michael J. Fox, diagnosed with Parkinson's disease at the height of his career, said, "Acceptance doesn't mean resignation. It means understanding that it is what it is and there's got to be a way through it." He has used this mindset to channel his energy into creating a remarkable life rather than remaining entrenched in anger and resentment of the facts.

We've both consistently received feedback from clients and colleagues that understanding the concept of what is, although not easy, opened them up to significant shifts in perception. Helene, a teacher and coaching client of Donna's, was distraught over the election. She was adamant in her refusal to accept Trump as president and began to experience sleeplessness, anxiety, and a short temper with those around her. She used to laugh often and easily, but noticed she was not laughing or enjoying herself as frequently. She recognized that she had been in adamant denial of Trump's being president. By choosing to accept that he had, in fact, won the electoral college vote and had indeed become president, she was able to look at things as they are and decide how she wished to proceed. She concluded that she would become a watchdog and hold Trump accountable for every action he took that would be harmful to children. She made it her mission to stay on top of news, bills, and anything else that came up that would be detrimental to them; she began to educate others; she coordinated postcard and phone campaigns to keep pressure on Trump, the administration, and Congress. She proudly stepped into her role as a warrior for justice and member of the resistance. Helene still experiences moments of outrage, disgust, and depression, but she is no longer swallowed up by them. Empowered, committed, and strong, she enthusiastically puts her energies into a movement that is fighting for change, not stuck fighting the reality of what is.

As a final note, we'd like to suggest that you read this section several times and take the time to fully internalize the concept of what is. It requires some practice, but the more you choose to accept the facts, the easier you will find it to shift from victim to powerhouse.

## Why *Beyond Resistance*?

If you have picked up this book, it is not an accident. You likely wish to remain vigilant and engaged, to be the change you wish to

*Introduction*

see in the world, but in a way that better works for you.

If you read this book thoroughly and take the time to work your way through the included exercises, we are confident you will have a clearer and healthier response to Trump, his administration, and his supporters. *Beyond Resistance* is written for both political observers and activists alike. Portions more specifically target one group or another, but each concept is a valuable tool useful to all.

By harnessing our energy, both negative and positive, and using it as effectively as possible, we will prevail. How we receive and respond to information matters if we expect to cope with the stress of the political roller-coaster on which we find ourselves. We must understand ourselves and others more deeply, organize and prioritize, and practice self-care. Without a determined and thought-out approach to each of these subjects, we will face an uphill battle as we work toward the results we desire.

Our goals in writing this book are:

- ▶ To provide effective tools and bring new perspectives to light that will help you cope with the stress and overwhelm of Trump

- ▶ To provide a deeper understanding of why you have the intense feelings and reactions you do

- ▶ To navigate some of the major roadblocks that hold you back in your resistance and life

- ▶ To help you identify what is most important to you and

create a plan of action to achieve your goals and take care of yourself in the process

- ▶ To provide insight as to why Trump supporters are as ardent and committed as they are (and no, it's not because they are all stupid)

- ▶ To provide the skills to clearly listen for, hear, and trust your inner voice so that you no longer need constant validation from others

- ▶ To demonstrate that self-care is neither self-indulgent nor selfish—it is critical.

## The Bottom Line

It is our deepest desire that you learn to manage the stress of the political deluge you face on a day-to-day basis. If you are an advocate or activist, *Beyond Resistance* will support you in staying emotionally, physically, and spiritually healthy so that you remain engaged at this critical time in our history. We want you to own and witness your brilliance come alive and to gain a deeper understanding of the unique contribution you were put on this earth to make. If your energy starts to diminish because you are overwhelmed, stressed, or spinning your wheels, it serves no one. You are a vital part of the resistance and the direction we move in as a nation. We need you at your best. And if you are an observer, you will learn how to manage the stress of the day's news and remain healthy as you stay informed.

*Introduction*

We recommend you find a journal that you love and use it while reading *Beyond Resistance.* If you commit to do the work laid out in this book, you will experience a reduction in your stress levels and an increase in your effectiveness as an observer or activist.

Now, let's get started.

CHAPTER 1

# Mirror, Mirror, on the Wall

The concepts of shadow and projection are critical and intertwined components of the work we do as coaches. It is valuable to talk about them in the context of today's political environment because they are vital to understanding the election, our intense emotional reactions, and the current political climate. You can apply shadow and projection concepts throughout your life, and we cannot overstate their importance, but for the purpose of *Beyond Resistance*, we talk about them in relation to the election and its aftermath.

## Shadow

Let's begin with shadow. The concept of shadow was introduced by the renowned Swiss psychologist and psychiatrist Carl Jung, who founded analytical psychology. According to Jung, your shadow is anything that you subconsciously believe about yourself or the world around you ("I'm not good enough," "The world isn't a safe place," "People are mean," etc.) as well as anything you cannot or will not accept about yourself and either consciously or subconsciously try to hide or suppress ("I'm stupid," "I'm lazy," "I'm greedy," etc.).

We have no shadows at birth, no beliefs, nothing hidden, nothing suppressed, but from an early age we attribute meaning to our experiences and to the words and behaviors of our adults and caretakers, interpreting them as meaning something, often negative, about us or the world. We come to believe that certain aspects of ourselves (that we are loud, wild, talkative, greedy, egotistical, thin-skinned, etc.) are or might be "bad" or unacceptable, and that we might lose the love of others and no longer be taken care of, or possibly even be hurt, if we exhibit them. Not all qualities we reject are what one would normally describe as negative; some may be considered positive: leadership, confidence, expressiveness, outspokenness. But, again, we may learn that they are not desirable either. We may be told not to be bossy when we exhibit our leadership or that we are full of ourselves when we demonstrate confidence. We reject these qualities and do whatever we must to not be "that." And what is the best way to show what you aren't? Hide the trait and show the world that you are the exact opposite. How do you prove to the world that you are not greedy? By making sure to show how generous you are! Not selfish? Put yourself last! Not a leader? Stay small and stifle your wisdom, voice, and creativity!

The problem with rejecting any part of yourself is that you lose the ability to be authentic. You become more concerned with proving what you want people to believe about you than with being who you actually are. You are in a constant battle, expending tremendous amounts of energy in hiding a part of yourself, in wearing a mask. You carry shame for what you subconsciously perceive as flaws in your makeup. You don't allow people to see you for who you really are, making real and honest connection with others difficult. How honest can a relationship be if you are not living in or communicating from an authentic place? And while you don't recognize this happening, it becomes a part of who you are on the deepest levels. You carry these subconscious beliefs and behaviors into adulthood where they play out in a variety of self-sabotaging ways.

Donna was raised by a mother who berated and hit her. The experience left her with the belief that she was bad and unlovable, judgments which were devastating to her. Donna hated the part of her mother that she determined was a "mean, nasty bitch" and made a subconscious promise to herself that she would never be like that. She also believed that if she was "bad," she would not be loved. To combat all of these perceived negative qualities, Donna set out to prove how good, sweet, kind, and compassionate she was. In the process, her life force was drained, and she was exhausted from wearing a mask, trying to make sure the world saw her as she wished to be seen. The end result was that Donna often said yes when she meant no, was taken advantage of, and hid from any kind of spotlight to ensure no one ever saw these "disgraceful" parts of her. Donna's life turned around when she learned about shadow and projection...stay tuned.

One of the easiest and most common ways to identify your shadows is to look at what you project onto others. Projection occurs as you come across people who "reflect back" a trait you subconsciously suppress in yourself. When this occurs, you become intensely reactive—we call it triggered. They may as well be holding up a big flashing neon sign with the name of the very thing you work so hard not to be—the rejected trait that you don't want to acknowledge in yourself. Your button has been pushed, and it is nearly impossible not to react. When you are triggered by someone, it is almost certainly because you are projecting a suppressed part of yourself onto them. And this trait that you find so offensive in them is your shadow, the quality you have rejected in yourself. In order to become whole, you will need to go through the process of finding acceptance of it.

Here's the catch: your tendency will be to say, "I'm not like that!" and dismiss the notion that it is a part of you. But we promise you that it is. How do we know? Because you are human and as such, possess every quality. You don't want to see or acknowledge this one because you have spent a lifetime working endlessly to prove otherwise to the world. We are both often met with emphatic defensiveness from our clients, and have heard more times than we can count, "That's not me. I could never be like that!" This is our clue that there is a shadow lurking beneath the surface begging to be acknowledged. In twelve-step programs, there is a saying: "If you can spot it, you've got it." We ask you to openheartedly explore and look for a time when you might have exhibited the very trait that you find so abhorrent.

We must mention that there is a difference between simply noticing something about another person and getting upset and worked up by it. If you are simply noticing, you are not projecting, but when you are worked up, you are. Feeling triggered by another person may be incredibly anger-provoking and stressful, but it is actually an opportunity to step into greater authenticity and freedom in your life. You will be amazed by the liberation you experience when you are released from the chains of needing to prove anything or have others believe something about you. It is like one hundred pounds being lifted from you.

Donna previously would become triggered by anyone she perceived as bad or a mean, nasty bitch. She learned that this was projection, and that moving beyond it would require her to look for where she might have been those things in the past or could be in the future. She would need to find the positive aspects or benefits to these qualities and get used to the fact that she could, indeed, at times be a bad person or a mean, nasty bitch, and that it was okay. You may be asking yourself, "How can being bad or a mean, nasty, bitch ever possibly be okay?" Think about a circumstance where being a mean, nasty bitch might be to your benefit. Imagine facing sexual harassment at work but being rebuffed when you report it. Is this a situation where being a mean, nasty bitch may be useful or necessary to call attention to the problem? Now take a moment to contemplate a situation where being bad might be a positive thing. Perhaps someone who works for a manufacturing company finds out that it is engaged in illegal dumping of toxic materials. While stealing company documents might be considered bad, in this case would being bad perhaps avert an environmental or health disaster? Is this a case where being bad might be good? And if standing up and fighting Trump requires you to be bad, would that be a time to put that quality to good use?

When you can see the positive aspects of any quality you have previously rejected, it is easier to accept that it is a part of you. When you can acknowledge that an attribute might benefit you in certain situations, you will no longer need to reject it or become triggered by it in others. In fact, you may not even notice it anymore! Once Donna learned about shadow and the value of embracing all parts of herself, she allowed herself to be fully seen. At that point, she stepped into her dreams of teaching, singing with John Denver (whom she had always admired), and making a difference in the lives of others through coaching. And, rest assured, her mean, nasty bitch side is alive and well today, being put to good use in the resistance.

Chris, a client of Kathy's, was raised by a workaholic father who could not relax. His dad left for work before Chris woke up for school and often got home after he was asleep. Weekends were never for fun, only yardwork or household chores. Anytime Chris would relax in his room or simply watch television, his dad looked at him with disdain and accused him of being lazy and pathetic. Chris's dad obviously had a belief that it was bad to be unproductive and taught that to Chris, who learned that he should avoid being seen as lazy or pathetic at all costs. Chris became a driven workaholic like his father and lacked joy in his life. He had difficulty sustaining intimate relationships because he didn't put time into nurturing them. He had insomnia from thinking about work at night, and his health was deteriorating because he didn't take time to exercise or eat well. However, none of this mattered to him as long as he wasn't seen as lazy or pathetic.

Following Trump's election, Chris noticed his irritation with people who called themselves members of the resistance but who, in his view, were not doing nearly enough. He described them as lazy and pathetic and was triggered each time he was confronted with them. Chris got to a point where he knew his life wasn't working for him and made the decision to work with a life coach. He learned about shadow and projection (among other topics) and worked through much of what had previously kept him feeling stuck and trapped. Chris is now rarely resentful of others and much less judgmental. He is happier and more at peace; puts less pressure on himself; and takes time to relax, exercise, and eat well. He has a girlfriend, and he is not triggered by others nearly as often.

You may wonder if a personality trait that is verifiable in another is still a projection. Projection is not about the quality itself as much as it is about your reaction to it. We can verify that Donald Trump is a liar. Glenn Kessler, who writes the popular "Fact Checker" column for the *Washington Post*, states that as of September 2017, Trump had made over one thousand false statements since becoming President. Does that make Trump horrifyingly uninformed—or a liar? We will leave that decision to you, but our point is that it is about your reaction to whatever trait you assign to him, not whether your assessment is true or false. If you are triggered, you are in projection and there is some self-exploration to be done.

The Buddhist teaching of interdependence tells us that people we perceive as our greatest enemies can be our greatest teachers because they show aspects of ourselves that we find unpalatable and give us the chance to heal. We need all of who we are and not just the parts we deem "positive." The idea of finding Trump within ourselves was echoed by James S. Gordon, a psychiatrist and founder of the Center for Mind-Body Medicine. In *The Guardian*, he writes, "Trump's grand and vulgar self-absorption is inviting all of us to examine our own selfishness. His ignorance calls us to attend to our own blind spots. The fears that he stokes and the isolation he promotes goad us to be braver, more generous."

Jeff Malone of Lumen Worldwide, a spiritually based personal growth organization, writes, "Trump, as the American Shadow, is projected on in one way or another by both detractors and supporters. Those who can't be with their dishonest, manipulative, racist, misogynistic, judgmental, or ignorant selves get triggered by what they see in Trump. Those who can't or won't be with their strong, successful, bold, decisive, independent selves see Trump as a hero who is above the law and doesn't need to be accountable for his actions. In either case, the challenge is for us to reclaim these parts and recognize where they show up in our lives so that we can heal and come back to wholeness. Only then can we see Trump clearly for who he truly is without our projection muddying the waters." He continues, "To stop being affected emotionally, you will need to make peace with the qualities that stir up such strong emotions in you. And how do you do this? By finding the valuable purpose in every quality that triggers you. Every quality you've rejected, and then projected, serves some purpose. Finding that value allows you to reclaim this quality and own it—freeing you from being triggered by it in others."

What qualities do you become triggered by when you look at Trump and his supporters? Do you regard them as crazy, unfit, arrogant, ignorant, deranged, mean-spirited, spiteful, or immature? We could go on but let's leave it at that! The good news is that this is the perfect opportunity for you to become more whole and authentic. By naming the personality trait that you find so disturbing in another person, you can begin to find acceptance for it and free yourself from its clutches. Where are you projecting on Trump and his followers? What do you see in them that you cannot bear to acknowledge in yourself?

### Shadow and Projection Journaling Exercise

This exercise will help you identify some of your shadows and projections. Answer the following questions in your journal:

- ▸ What personality trait do you most love about yourself? Is it your brilliance, your generosity, your creativity?

- ▸ What is the opposite of this quality? Would it be stupidity, selfishness, or dullness? That opposite quality is your shadow.

- ▸ Think about someone in your life or in the world whom you abhor and cannot bear.

- ▸ What is the personality trait that most upsets you about that person? That is another shadow.

- ▸ Choose one of these traits and see if you can find it within yourself.

- ▶ Imagine a scenario where this perceived negative quality could provide value.

- ▶ Acknowledge the possible benefits of this quality and affirm that you no longer need to reject it or deny it is a part of you.

- ▶ Visualize releasing your fear of this quality so that you no longer need to project it on others.

## The Bottom Line

Many of our clients affirm that an understanding of shadow and projection enormously changes their lives for the better. They describe these as concepts that let them off the leash of ongoing reactivity to their outer world. There is a lot of projection going on in our country at the moment. We are projecting all over each other and the president, creating a huge chasm and deep animosity. We cannot afford to allow this to continue as we all pay too high a price. We who are committed to our democracy would do well to understand these concepts and begin the process of healing.

CHAPTER 2

# I Just Can't Take It Anymore!

We are going to wager a guess that if you are politically engaged, you are at least marginally overwhelmed by the current political climate. Donna notices she gets tired, frenzied, and indecisive. Kathy likens her overwhelm to spinning out of control; she makes more mistakes and doesn't get a lot done. People handle overwhelm in their own ways, and we were curious as to how our friends were coping. We asked and got some pretty creative answers:

- Avoidance and Rachel Maddow
- Watching CNN and hearing commentators validate that Trump is bat-shit crazy
- Wine
- Xanax
- Andy Borowitz, political satirist
- Spending a lot of time on anything remotely funny or amusing

- Carbohydrates

- Rainbow Randy, comedian (find him on YouTube)

- Using Twitter to vent

These are all great strategies, and we've used a few ourselves, but they are only short-term fixes. The accumulation of our day-to-day work, family, and social responsibilities, world events, and technology—and our inability to manage it—causes us all to become overwhelmed at one time or another. Right now, the stakes are even higher. We are bombarded daily with news and information about this administration that can easily overwhelm. It will require presence and mindfulness, as well as physical, emotional, and spiritual self-care to stay politically involved and healthy. None of us can afford to ignore ourselves and our needs if we are going to remain engaged for the long haul and effect real change.

Overwhelm is a sign. It's a big, glaring sign letting you know you are somehow not listening to yourself, not honoring yourself, not taking care of yourself properly. It is a notification that you are doing too much, taking on too much, or accepting too much responsibility. We call this being out of integrity with yourself.

There are usually early signs or clues that you are somehow out of integrity. You may notice an uncomfortable feeling in your head, chest, or belly. You might find yourself breaking promises, feeling resentful, or habitually compromising. These signs often begin as gentle whispers but continue to increase in their intensity if ignored. Ultimately, they will feel like a sledgehammer to the head, demanding your attention. Resistance member and refugee advo-

*I Just Can't Take It Anymore!*

cate Terri said yes to everything because it all seemed so critical. She believed that if she said no, she would be letting everybody down; she continued to take on more. Terri became anxious and began to make careless mistakes at work. She was tired but told herself she had to keep going. After a while, her stomach bothered her, but she claimed not to have time to go to the doctor. Instead, she popped antacids. Terri was doing it all—writing postcards, making calls, organizing and showing up to protest, attending local activist group meetings and taking on further responsibility there. The inevitable day came when Terri could not get out of bed because of acute stomach pain. A friend drove her to the ER where she was diagnosed with an ulcer and exhaustion. Of course, in hindsight, we could see the warning signs. Terri did not listen to her body or act in integrity with its needs. Had she paid attention to the early clues and taken care of herself, she might have saved a lot of pain, time, money, and loss of productivity.

Kathy's client Jessica also neglected signs that she was out of integrity with herself when she began dating Jonathan. They had fun and enjoyed each other, but there was a little tug inside Jessica warning her that Jonathan was overly self-centered. Jessica wanted things to work. She had been single for a while and wanted desperately to be in a relationship. Because of this she ignored the red flags and her inner voice. Jonathan often made plans without consulting her and rarely asked her about her thoughts, needs, or desires. Jessica made excuses for him, but in her heart she knew the relationship was not working for her. When she tried to share her feelings with Jonathan, she was met with resistance and deflection; he told her it was her problem, and she backed down again and again. Jessica believed a breakup would be too painful and would require starting over again. She dreaded both of these outcomes and continued to let things go, question herself, and make excuses for Jonathan's behavior. She told herself he had many other good qualities, he was trying his best, no one is perfect, and everyone must put up with things in a partner that are not ideal. But underneath, Jessica felt ashamed of her willingness to accept what she knew in her heart was unacceptable to her. She pulled away from friends and began to isolate. Things got worse and Jessica was unhappy, but the fear of leaving kept her stuck.

One day, a year into the relationship, Jonathan came home and announced that he had been offered a job in another city and had decided to take it. She expressed her feelings about not being considered in this major decision but was met with indifference. The relationship abruptly ended. The pain Jessica suffered at that point was immense. She had given her time, heart, and energy to a relationship that she knew all along was not right for her. She ignored the signs and her inner knowing and made excuses to stay safe, but in the end, had nowhere left to hide from the truth: Jonathan was more interested in himself than in Jessica or their relationship. She had been out of integrity with herself from the beginning, and it resulted in the loss of more than a relationship—it cost Jessica her self-esteem. Kelley Kosow, CEO of The Ford Institute and author of *The Integrity Advantage*, writes, "Every time you bite your tongue, you swallow your integrity." If Jessica had made choices in alignment with her instincts from the beginning, she would have saved herself the pain of the relationship and the heartache of its demise.

Fortunately, the more you practice listening to, trusting, and acting on your internal voice, the less likely it is you will have the sledgehammer-to-the-head experience. Awareness of the fact that you perpetuate shame and self-sabotaging behavior when you are out of integrity, and gaining skills to return to integrity, are life-changers. Learning to recognize the inner whispers that you are out of integrity, and cultivating the desire and ability to make adjustments immediately, will create a shift in your life. When you begin to respect yourself more by living in integrity, not only will you notice you have greater self-confidence and self-love, but you will also find that others treat you with more respect. Integrity is a journey, not a destination. It is a learning process, and it is important to remember that you need not seek perfection.

When you are overwhelmed and trying to keep your head above water, it's a sure bet that you are in need of a check-in, a sign that you are out of integrity. It is precisely in these times that you are offered an invaluable roadmap to self-discovery and understanding.

Debbie Ford once asked: "If you are in overwhelm, where are you out of integrity?" Most of us believe that when we are overwhelmed, it is because of factors outside of us or beyond our control, but this thinking is misguided. While every indicator may point to the outer world, the source of your overwhelm is within you. Only you can determine what is best for you, what your needs are, and what are healthy boundaries.

The positive side to overwhelm is that it can serve as a catalyst for change, greater self-awareness, and self-care. It is an opportunity to return to integrity. When overwhelm sets in, we usually make it mean something negative about us, that we are less-than or inadequate, and use it as an opportunity to beat ourselves up. This berating only adds to overwhelm and we fall even deeper into the rabbit hole of shame and blame, perpetuating the cycle.

> *Most of us feel a little crazy from time to time. Periods of high stress can make us feel like we're losing it, as can being surrounded by people whose values are very different from our own. The main purpose of the wake-up call that feeling crazy provides is to let us know that something in our lives is out of balance. Confirm for yourself that you are capable of creating a sane and peaceful reality for yourself. Try to remember that most people have felt, at one time or another, that they are losing it.*
> —Madyson Taylor, co-founder of *Daily Om*

Overwhelm is a message to yourself from yourself, a call to action, a sign to pay greater attention to your needs and what you can comfortably manage and have the desire to manage. One common source of overwhelm is comparing yourself to others. This usually leads to feelings of inadequacy which then drive you to take on more and more responsibility and commitments, subconsciously hoping to alleviate your discomfort and prove—to yourself and others—that you are good enough. For political observers, this may mean telling yourself others are more informed or smarter than you. Activists may believe others are doing more or are more effective in their activism. But unless you are a competitive athlete, this kind of

*I Just Can't Take It Anymore!*

self-comparison is a losing proposition. True well-being is about you and your relationship with yourself; it can only be achieved by taking the time to check in, get clear, and make choices based on your priorities. Being in or noticing overwhelm is not the problem—not acting or taking responsibility for it is. When overwhelm owns you, you have lost.

How do you know if you are in overwhelm? Some of the warning signs are:

- Numbing out with food, alcohol, social media, work, etc.
- Sleeping too much or too little
- Feeling out of control or powerless
- Forgetting or losing things
- Experiencing heart palpitations or a general sense of anxiety
- Retreating from friends, family, or the world
- Acting reckless or careless
- Jumping to conclusions
- Being unable to focus
- Making excuses, blaming others, or painting yourself as a victim
- Having a short temper, angering easily

- Wanting to cry or scream from frustration
- Lacking follow-through
- Feeling stuck
- Not taking care of yourself
- Being self-centered

## The Overwhelm Quiz

Rate each question on a scale from 1-5, with 1 being the least true and 5 being the truest.

My workdays and weekends are jam-packed.

When spending time with my friends, family, partner, I'm anxious to move on to the next thing—I can never fully enjoy the moment.

Quiet time for myself seems impossible.

I use my vacation days to run errands and catch up on chores.

I manage to stay on top of things, but I don't know how long I can keep up.

More often than not, I am tired and stressed out.

My life is certainly not boring, but it's also wearing me down.

I find myself waking up angry, scared, or upset.

I tend to say "yes" to every request.

Even when I have time for myself, I'm not doing anything that nourishes or replenishes my physical, emotional, or spiritual well-being.

**Scoring**

If you scored between 10 and 15, you are doing great!

If you scored between 16 and 30, you may want to think about ways to take a little more time for yourself or use your time to support your well-being more effectively.

If you scored between 30 and 50, take heed and consider your self-care now!

# Anger

Emotions play a large role in overwhelm. Anger and fear, while catalysts for resistance, can also hinder productivity and even one's love for humanity. For example, when we are angry or afraid, we tend to focus on our anger or fear to the exclusion of all else. This focus impedes our ability to use our energy in positive ways. Trust and safety are the greatest fuel for productivity. When in anger or fear, we feel neither. Think about it: if you are constantly worried that your boss will criticize you at work, will you produce your best work? If you are continually ruminating about Trump's potential next move, are you pushing people away, seeing only the negative in others, or acting from a place of hate rather than love? In the spirit of full disclosure, we admit that we have both been in that dark place, and it left us powerless and unproductive.

> *While anger can bring about change, it can ultimately lead only to more conflict. This is true both in our personal lives and in the fate of a nation.*
> —Brother Thầy Pháp Dung, Buddhist monk

Because you are a human being, we are willing to wager that you have experienced anger at some point in your life. It is a part of all of us, and if you don't believe it, think about your reaction when you broke something, burned yourself, were cut off on the road, or even read a Trump tweet!

Although anger is a natural part of our make-up, we often use our anger as an excuse to beat ourselves up, believing it is "bad" to be angry. In truth, we are best served when we don't condemn ourselves or others for any feeling, including anger. We need all our emotions if we are to be whole human beings. But we reject our anger because it frightens us. Most of us have had anger used against us at one time or another and have become fearful of it. We are afraid of anger directed toward us as well as our anger toward others. Women have an especially difficult time dealing with their anger; we are taught by society that it is unladylike, that we should be sweet and quiet, that we should hold in our rage because it makes us ugly. However, according to the American Psychological Association, there are costs to internalized anger: depression, health problems, and communication difficulties, among others. There are those who believe that because so many in our country felt unheard, unseen, and left behind, a tsunami of anger was unleashed that had long festered beneath the surface, leading to Trump's election.

Donna is on the board of directors of Challenge Day, an organization with a vision that every child is safe, loved, and celebrated for being exactly who he or she is. One of Challenge Day's core concepts is that of the internal balloon. Imagine that you have a balloon inside you and, as life brings you losses, failures, disappointments, and betrayals, your balloon slowly fills up. If you are afraid of your emotions, or somehow believe they are bad, and are unwilling to deal with them—in other words, if you are afraid to deal with what's inside your balloon—your anger will leak out, mostly onto those you love, and impede your ability to create successful and happy relationships, including the one with yourself. If not dealt with, your balloon will eventually pop and you'll find yourself spiraling out of control. Holding in emotions is a no-win situation.

We teach our clients that emotions are neither inherently bad nor inherently good. They are simply emotions, and it is how we use them and what we tell ourselves about them that matters most. For example, anger about Trump may motivate you to take action or find a voice that you didn't, wouldn't, or couldn't express before. Using your anger might lead to places you never imagined or believed possible. An example of this is our anger leading us to become authors! There is a time and place where every emotion can serve you. Allow yourself to affirm that you no longer need to fear your anger or make it "wrong." And when you no longer have the need to shut off any part of yourself, you will find greater wholeness and freedom.

> *You should be angry. You must not be bitter. Bitterness is like cancer. It eats upon the host. It doesn't do anything to the object of its displeasure. So use that anger. You write it. You paint it. You dance it. You march it. You vote it. You do everything about it. You talk it. Never stop talking it.*
> —Maya Angelou, author

Donna used her anger as an opportunity to let her voice be heard and counted when Senate Majority Leader Mitch McConnell talked about the Democrats' planned filibuster of Trump's Supreme Court nominee, Neil Gorsuch. McConnell claimed he wasn't obstructionist, but the Democrats were. After what Donna considered eight years of Republican obstructionism, a behavior that was openly acknowledged by McConnell himself as a flat-out goal at every turn during Obama's presidency, she was overwhelmed with anger and frustration at this twisted version of her reality and with the attempt to revise history and spin facts. It brought her to tears. She felt powerless and frustrated over this mischaracterization and experienced something akin to mental paralysis.

Donna says: "It was good no one was home with me because, boy, did I let it go! I gave voice to my anger (I literally screamed into my pillow!) and started the process of releasing it by evaluating how I could use the tools I have to let the anger fuel me rather than hold me back. The truth is that I really wanted to go to bed and pull the covers over my head, which would have been fine had it been a conscious decision, but in this case, it would have been an excuse not to deal with my feelings."

*I Just Can't Take It Anymore!*

Donna thought about what she could do to use her anger to further her goals. She decided to write a postcard to Senator McConnell, a message that gave her a sense of empowerment as she let her voice be heard in a way other than screaming into her pillow. She sat down to work on this book as an outlet for her heightened emotions, channeling them to further her goals. She chose to take positive steps instead of shutting down or hiding and letting anger and overwhelm win.

Unbridled anger exacts a price if we do not have the knowledge or tools to turn it around and use it to move our mission and goals forward as Donna did. Living in a perpetual state of anger and upheaval is not healthy for anyone. It is nearly impossible to maintain your emotional, physical, and spiritual well-being, not to mention your stamina, in this state. Anger is a valuable catalyst and motivator for action, but it will wear you down and diminish your effectiveness in all things. You don't need to be in continual tumult to effect change. Greenpeace is a fine example of using anger for good. Members take their anger and peacefully stand between Japanese whaling ships and the ships' targets to protect our environment. The Women's March is another example of collective anger turned into something positive: a movement that furthers a sense of unity, love, and empowerment. The energy of anger is powerful, and if it is used productively, it can lead to impressive, unimagined results.

Our friend Justin was distraught over the election and what he saw and heard during the transition and after the inauguration. He spent much of each day angry and finger-pointing. He released his anger by going on social media several times a day and ranting. He wanted to make sure everyone knew how dreadful it all was (as if they didn't know already!), and how much it enraged him. Perhaps his outrage would inspire people to get involved politically, but that wasn't enough. Justin realized he wasn't doing anything positive to effect change and he began to notice that his anger was affecting his relationships. He was unsettled and people were becoming oversaturated and unresponsive to him. Justin reevaluated his goals and approach and decided to make a shift.

Rather than post about what was wrong and put negative energy into the world and his own psyche, he decided to highlight the positive. He would share positive actions people could take rather than be a source of more angst. When an elected official took a stand, or a company or private individual took effective action, Justin shared it and suggested that people acknowledge or thank them. People immediately responded to this shift. They began replying to and sharing his posts and thanking him. This propelled him even further in his activism by creating more positive energy within and around him.

*A positive attitude causes a chain reaction of positive thoughts, events, and outcomes. It is a catalyst and it sparks extraordinary results.*
—Wade Boggs, 1996 World Series Champion

The choice is yours. Will you acknowledge your anger and use it to your advantage or deny, be ashamed of, or be overtaken by it and allow it to function as a roadblock that keeps you from becoming all you are meant to be?

## Fear

Beneath anger lies fear—both real and imagined. Many of us are frightened right now—frightened that truth and justice are no longer part of our democracy. We are terrified that a crazy person is in the White House and neither he nor his Cabinet members are acting "normally" or even sanely.

We are a divided nation—each side operating from a place of distrust and trepidation. The issue of gun ownership is a perfect example. Democrats fear the rampant proliferation of guns and gun violence while Republicans fear their Second Amendment rights will be stripped from them. We are so focused on what we are afraid of that we can't understand the perspective or fears of others, making compassion and dialogue nearly impossible.

After Trump ordered the bombing of a Syrian air base in April 2017, we were both overcome with anger and confusion. Our minds raced, we experienced a heaviness in our chests, and our stomachs were in knots. We explored the deeper causes of our responses, searching for what specifically was triggering us—it was fear.

Donna discovered her fear that the childish and impetuous behavior of the leader of the free world would drive us to World War Three. She described Trump as the little boy who has nuclear weapons. "He's on the same level as North Korean leader Kim Jong Un. He is fully capable of starting World War III on a whim. We'll all be annihilated." It is natural that, subconsciously fearing nuclear annihilation, Donna would experience a strong emotional response!

Kathy recognized that much of her fear stemmed from the story she created that Trump's egoism, narcissism, and lack of impulse control would start a war and that her teenage son would be drafted. She laid her greatest fear—that something would happen to her child—on top of her beliefs about Trump and created a terrifying scenario in her mind. By recognizing what was driving some of her most intense emotions, she was able to take a step back and call forth a little more objectivity, which brought her back from blind panic and overwhelm. She recognized that she could take positive action that would help her, her son, and the world. Or she could be taken down by her emotions.

Our emotional responses are triggered by the story we tell ourselves about any given situation—in other words, the meanings we attach. It is what we tell ourselves that has the greatest bearing on our reactions and feelings. We may not be able to change what is happening in our external world, but we can change what is happening internally and find ourselves in a more emotionally balanced place. Donna initially made the Syrian situation mean we would face a world war and possible nuclear annihilation. She took stock and, although still highly concerned, pulled herself together by acknowledging that Trump has experienced and knowledgeable national security advisors surrounding him. While she may not have agreed with them all politically, she trusted that they were voices of reason. She chose to put her faith in them; doing so allowed her to feel calmer and opened the door for focus and action to return.

*I Just Can't Take It Anymore!*

One way to avoid the cycle of emotional overwhelm is to make the conscious decision not to descend into negativity about every upsetting thing we read or hear. Negativity saps our power and robs us of energy and possibility. One day, as we discussed remarks Trump had made about Palestinians and Israelis getting along well, we ended up devolving into "He's such a moron" in about ten seconds. We both noticed the negativity in our bodies—Donna in her chest, Kathy in her stomach. We recognized that acknowledging what we read or heard and moving on without a hair-on-fire reaction or absorbing the emotional component helped protect us from the emotional, physical, and spiritual fallout. It can do the same for you.

Donna's friend Lauren recently shared that she wakes up with "morning frights." She, like most of us, is worried our rights are being eroded by those in power who fear losing their status. To help combat her anxiety, Lauren decided that she would join a group of like-minded local women with whom she could talk and share her thoughts and feelings. She says, "Sometimes we all need support from others. Just expressing my fear and knowing I have support helps calm me down."

> *I will always have fears, but I need not be my fears, for*
> *I have other places within myself from which to speak and act.*
> —Parker J. Palmer, author, educator, and activist

Stay open to your feelings; they are clues. Don't try to shut them out. In chaos, fear, or distraction, it is difficult to achieve goals or process information in a clearheaded and objective way. The time we lose to overwhelm could be used to make a positive difference. Is the wheel-spinning and ruminating serving you, or is it keeping you stuck?

## The Bottom Line

Overwhelm can manifest in many forms, but it is always a signal that we are not taking effective care of ourselves. Overwhelm is part of the human condition and something we can use to our benefit if we pause, expose its source, and take action to readjust our patterns and choices. It provides us an opportunity to bring ourselves into greater integrity. As a final note, be careful not to use overwhelm—or any emotion—as an excuse to tune out and shut down. Remain vigilant and prioritize listening to yourself: living a life of integrity is the best safeguard against overwhelm.

CHAPTER 3

# I Gotta Be Honest

Merriam-Webster's online dictionary defines integrity as "the quality or state of being complete or undivided: completeness." In ethics, integrity is regarded as the honesty and truthfulness or accuracy of one's actions, acting in alignment with one's values. It is our moral compass. When we live in personal integrity, we are present and honest with ourselves and the world around us. We are attuned, listening deeply to our truth and making choices from that place. The resistance is, in fact, a movement born of personal integrity.

When living in integrity with yourself, you are whole and complete because you have no need to hide any part of yourself, seek validation from others, or compartmentalize your life—there is one you, consistent in all areas. When you are in integrity, there is peace within. This does not mean everything is easy or simple, but rather, an underlying ease and a connectedness with yourself, others, and life is present.

Personal integrity is not about being right or wrong or judging others for being right or wrong—in fact, judgment of others is a sign that you are out of integrity. Rather, it is something within us and unique to every individual. Living in integrity looks different for each person; integrity is what Debbie Ford refers to as your inner balance scale. Only you can determine what is in integrity for you and what isn't. Donna realized that keeping her mouth shut when she wanted to speak out was not in integrity for her. She recognized this by noticing the anger and frustration she felt each time it occurred. Kathy, in her attempts not to be arrogant, a shadow she desperately wanted to hide from the world, felt pressure in her body each time she made herself small in order to gain the approval or love of others.

How do you know when you are out of integrity? When your scales are out of balance, there are signs, and once you learn to identify and trust them, you have the opportunity to take action to bring yourself back into balance. Each person's internal warning system is different. You may notice a nagging voice questioning what you are doing, or you may experience a physical nudge, such as a knot in your stomach, rapid heartbeat, or fatigue. You may feel a dizzy swirling sensation in your head, or a less-specific sense of unease. You may have emotional discomfort—a feeling of being stuck, helpless, hollow, alone, or disconnected. Or perhaps you have trouble sleeping, ruminate on a particular subject over and over again, or have difficulty with concentration or focus.

Whatever signs appear, it is important to listen to their messages because they will not go away and will distract you from what is most important to you. Kathy shares a recent experience of being called to stand in personal integrity when she heard a racist remark. She recalls, "A contractor was at my house and made a comment about a particular minority group. I felt nauseated and my mind raced. Letting it pass may have seemed like the easier choice, but I knew in the long run it would not be—that I would carry the shame of not speaking up and be upset with myself. I spoke up, told the contractor that I was offended and uncomfortable with what he said, and suggested that he may want to be more careful in the future. He was taken aback and apologized, and I hope he will think twice the next time. I left the encounter feeling at peace, knowing I stood up for what I believed was right."

The two of us have discussed whether it is in integrity to be caught up in the day-to-day minutiae of "Trump world"—what Trump does, says, tweets—when we have no control over his behavior and know that fixating on him is at the expense of our well-being. We concluded that it depends on how it impacts us. If we are able to simply observe, that is one thing. If we are triggered or taken over by our responses, it is worth evaluating whether this time spent is a benefit or a hindrance to our resistance and our lives.

Cliff Barry of Shadow Work Seminars, Inc., says, "Your impact is based on how much you are in alignment with your values." How might you bring yourself into greater integrity and become more impactful in your activism or ability to synthesize and respond to information? It is important to recognize and remember once again that there is no perfection—no human being is in integrity one hundred percent of the time—but the point is to use those times to learn, grow, and adjust. Your goal is to notice, listen to, and trust your inner voice; choose your course of action; and then act.

In the late 1970s, the phrase "living in truth" was playwright and author Václav Havel's hallmark. No single phrase did more to inspire those trying to subvert and overthrow the communist hold on Europe. In his essay "The Power of the Powerless," about the mind of the local greengrocer, Havel writes, "Just imagine that one day something in our greengrocer snaps and he begins to say what he really thinks at political meetings. And he even finds the strength in himself to express solidarity with those whom his conscience commands him to support. In this revolt the greengrocer steps out of living within the lie. He rejects the ritual and breaks the rules of the game. He discovers once more his suppressed identity and dignity. He gives his freedom a concrete significance. His revolt is an attempt to live within the truth." For each of us to find peace, there must come a time when we square our outward actions with our beliefs.

As you can see, integrity has a tremendous impact on your activism, political engagement, and life. When your scales are too far out of balance, an unexpected thing happens: you begin to punish yourself. There is a saying that the "guilty seek punishment," and in this case your guilt lies in not honoring yourself. The punishment can show up in a myriad of places and ways: in your relationships and work performance; in your dreams and goals, addictions, self-care and self-sabotage; and even as health or psychological issues.

Can you see where you may currently be out of integrity? Is there something you did or didn't do, said or didn't say, or even something you may have thought that was not in integrity for you? Did you take part in gossiping about or bad-mouthing someone? Did you agree to something you didn't feel good about? Did you tell someone a lie to protect yourself from their response? Have you been angry with a good friend, and, rather than have an honest conversation about your feelings, held it in and acted out? Did you say yes when you didn't want to or take on another responsibility when you knew you already had too much on your plate? Do you notice any discomfort or pangs of guilt letting you know that you somehow didn't act from your truth?

Living in personal integrity is not always the easy choice, but the payoff is nothing short of emotional freedom. If you want to learn who you are, or "find yourself," the surest way is to listen to and trust yourself and act accordingly—even when it seems impossible. It takes time and practice to develop and act on your internal warning system, but we promise you it is worth it.

The three fundamental steps that lead to a state of integrity are listening, trusting, and acting. In this chapter we focus on personal integrity with regard to political engagement, but remember that all concepts in this book can be applied to every area of your life.

## Step One: **Listen**

*See how nature—trees, flowers, grass—grows in silence;*
*see the stars, the moon and the sun, how they move in silence...*
*we need silence to be able to touch souls.*
—Mother Teresa of Calcutta, humanitarian

The source of all integrity is within. The universe continually sends us messages, which often begin as gentle whispers but grow incrementally louder until we pay heed. When we refuse to listen or take action, the messages swell until it feels like we've been hit by a Mack truck. Believe it or not, feeling "hit by a Mack truck" is in dictionary.com, where it's defined as "astonished; stunned; bowled over." How often have you felt stunned or bowled over by an outcome in your life? How many times were you surprised when something didn't happen the way you thought it should? If you trace back, perhaps you can identify a little voice that whispered in your ear or recall a gentle tapping on your shoulder that you ignored before you eventually ended up somewhere you never intended to go.

You may not have been taught to connect within—most of us weren't. Perhaps you have an inkling that there is something tugging at you but don't know what to do with the feeling, so you subconsciously look for ways to distract yourself from it. The distractions can be self-sabotaging behaviors, such as overworking, overspending, or wasting too much time on social media, or seemingly positive behaviors, such as exercising. You might have received the message that being quiet or still was lazy, self-centered, indulgent, or just plain ridiculous. So, you busy yourself or cut off from those little nudges and intuitions, negate and ignore them. Let's take a closer look at how to begin to tune in to ourselves.

> *Everyone who wills can hear their inner voice.*
> *It is within everyone.*
> —Mahatma Gandhi, social activist

We each possess an inner voice; it is not something we need to develop. We simply need to get better at hearing and trusting what it is saying to us. Your inner voice is already living inside you, waiting for you to pay attention. You need only practice the skills to hear it. Here are a few tips:

You have an inner voice that is always ready and willing to guide you if you take the time to listen. Now is the time to nurture and trust that inner voice. The more you practice being in silence, the louder your authentic inner voice becomes.

Let go of the belief that you must have all the answers and force life to happen your way. Usually life doesn't respond so readily or positively when you are in this controlling state. Can you let go and, in the words of Debbie Ford, "resign from being master of the universe"?

Be patient. (No, we did not say "become complacent.") Notice your thoughts and feelings as you begin to listen. Where are they coming from—fear (I don't know if I'm doing this right, it's taking too long, I don't know how, etc.) or love (I'm grateful for this opportunity to learn about myself, my path will unfold as it needs to, I'm exactly where I need to be right now, etc.)? Goodness knows, there are enough pressures in life...you don't need to add more!

Practice!

When you learn to be in the stillness, to listen, and to trust, it's as if something speaks to you on a soul level. You get an inkling, the subtlest of feelings, that something is motivating and moving you. You feel in flow with yourself and the universe, and it is nothing short of miraculous!

## Step Two: **Trust**

You probably notice a few different voices inside you, talking to you a good amount of the time, some with negativity and fear, others with clarity and peace. Initially, your inner wisdom may be frightening. It may even cause an internal firestorm of resistance coming from your defensive and protective self. Over time, as you become more trusting of the wisdom coming from within, you will find you are less reactive to and less afraid of what you hear. You will learn to recognize the part of you that tries to negate your truth and convince you that you are wrong, releasing you from its power. Truth doesn't always present itself right away; it takes practice to identify it. But if, after time, you are unsure whether you are hearing your true inner voice, you probably are not.

Constantly asking for the opinion of others, what they think you should say or do, if what you are thinking or being is "okay" is usually a signal that you are not tuned in to or trusting your inner wisdom. We are not talking about requesting specific input in areas where you may lack information or expertise, such as the best way to get an op-ed placed in your local newspaper, or hearing another's perspective, but rather, using others to avoid responsibility or create a safety net for yourself. Do you doubt yourself because the powers that be have different beliefs or ideas? In your heart, do you believe love is love and gay couples should have the right to marry, but your church and family have taken an immovable stance on the subject and caused you to question your instincts and perhaps stay silent out of fear of rejection or other response, such as anger or belittling? Have you taken on your family's beliefs and been afraid to speak out, even when they aren't in alignment with your own values, because you believe you *should* listen to your family elders? When you're in a should mindset, you lose the ability to be in balance.

## Integrity Introspection Process

We recommend reading the process below aloud and recording it on your phone, iPad, or other device, and then listening to it with your eyes closed. Or, you can listen to a recording of the process at *www.beyondresistancebook.com.* Allow it to guide you to a place of trust, safety, and sacredness within and, when prompted, write down your answer to each question in a journal. Use your breath throughout the exercise. It is your greatest transformational tool and one of the most effective ways to connect with your inner voice.

As you begin your process, allow yourself the freedom to experience it in whatever way it unfolds for you. There is no right or wrong—trust that your inner wisdom is always there, always present, always ready to guide you. At times, it may be obscured like the sun behind moving clouds, but it is always there for you.

- Take three slow, deep breaths—breathe in through your nose, breathe out through your mouth. Follow your breath and allow yourself to relax. Feel your body melting into your chair.
- Continue to breathe and keep your attention on your breath. Allow your breath to take you deeper inside and give yourself permission to release any concerns.
- Notice any thoughts or feelings that may be present and allow them to float by as though they were clouds in the sky.

- Continue with your breath and visualize yourself in a safe and protected space. It may be a place you have been before or somewhere in your imagination. It might be a room, a garden, or anywhere that is nurturing and peaceful for you.
- Notice the details of this beautiful space and visualize yourself there. What sounds do you hear? What are the scents, the colors? Is there water nearby or perhaps a forest? Are there birds or butterflies? Take a moment to immerse yourself in this place. Breathe into the safety of it and know that this is your sacred space where you have the wisdom of the universe.
- Now, in your imagination, find a comfortable place to sit—it may be on a chair, a bench, a grassy area, or a sandy beach. Take a seat and continue to focus on your breath, all the while trusting that you are safe, knowing that you have everything you need inside you. As you exhale, let go of anything that stands between you and that trust.
- Breathe in again and feel yourself connecting with your heart. Gently ask yourself, "Am I giving enough attention today to my emotional, spiritual, and physical well-being in response to my feelings about Trump?" Without pressure, take your time and allow yourself to listen for a simple yes or no arising easily from within.
- When you receive your answer, gently ask yourself whether there is anything specific you can do at the moment to further support your well-being. Again, breathe and listen for an answer without any pressure or judgment. Notice how it feels to be in this sacred space, deeply connected to yourself.
- Take a moment to thank your inner voice and acknowledge yourself for your courage in exploring something new. When you are

ready, allow yourself to open your eyes and come back to the room.

Wonderful! You just completed a simple exercise to begin the process of listening to and connecting with your inner voice. As a final step, you will want to decide whether to take action on anything that came to light during the process. It's important not to hurry or judge yourself or your progress—that only serves to keep you from reaching a place of trust and ease with yourself.

Practice this exercise daily for a few minutes, and, as you strengthen your connection within, you may begin to substitute other questions such as:

- ▶ What talents and gifts do I possess that will best serve the resistance? In which way might I put them to use?
- ▶ What do I need to do to help reduce my Trump-stress?
- ▶ What can I acknowledge myself for as a resistance member?

Learn to be comfortable in silence—feel for balance. You will know when you are there. Be patient and soon your inner wisdom will find its way to its own important questions. Be curious and honest with yourself. Have some fun and notice how your inner voice works.

## Step Three: **Act**

Listening and trusting your inner wisdom are important, but equally important is the decision to take action. You may notice that taking action is an ongoing theme throughout *Beyond Resistance*, because without action, thought and insight are merely fantasies. Knowing that it is critical to elect Democrats is great, but all the knowing in the world won't get them elected. If we don't get out and support campaigns, all the intentions and desires won't matter. We can have a million great ideas, but what do they amount to if we don't act upon them? The same holds true for your inner wisdom: you can hear it all day long, but if you don't take concrete action in alignment with its message, it will be virtually impossible to live in personal integrity.

> *What one does is what counts*
> *and not what one had the intention of doing.*
> —Pablo Picasso, artist

## The Bottom Line

Integrity plays an enormous role in who we are and, more specifically, how we resist. Getting clear on what's most important to you, creating a plan of action to get there (something we'll be covering later in this book), and following through—these are the life-changing choices that will lead you to a life of personal integrity. Remember, as is true with most things, integrity is not a destination but a journey. If you take it on from a place of curiosity, it is sure to be a journey filled with adventure and one that will lead you to a miraculous sense of peace, balance, and well-being.

CHAPTER 4

# Self-Care as a Revolutionary Act

*Caring for myself is not self-indulgence; it is self-preservation, and that is an act of political warfare.*
—Audre Lorde, author

In an article published in the *New England Journal of Medicine*, Professor David Williams of the Harvard T.H. Chan School of Public Health and Massachusetts General/McLean Hospital psychiatrist Morgan Medlock say that the side effects of the 2016 election may include everything from stress to "increased risk for disease, babies born too early, and premature death." According to the 2017 American Psychological Association's annual Stress in America: The State of Our Nation survey, nearly two-thirds of Americans (63 percent) say the future of the nation is a very or somewhat significant source of stress, slightly more than perennial stressors like money (62 percent) and work (61 percent). Doctors have told us of increased visits from patients with anxiety, gastrointestinal issues, and the like.

The election of Trump is making us sick: if we didn't know it from our own experience, we can now read about it from leading public health and psychiatric professionals. One of the primary reasons we wrote *Beyond Resistance* was our belief that if there was not a shift in our approach to Trump, there would be a public health crisis as the result of the extreme levels of stress and despair experienced by so many. Our training and experience have demonstrated the importance of self-care—physical, emotional, and spiritual—and boundary-setting as well as the benefits of clarity and integrity. We see how integral self-care is to effective engagement and activism. When we are flooded with overwhelming emotions and not nourishing our bodies or getting enough sleep, we can't think clearly, much less be at our best. The same is true if we are not spiritually or emotionally fit. We believe it is important, if not critical, to determine your "nonnegotiables"—the self-care practices that are at the top of your priority list and necessary in order for you to remain in integrity with yourself. We encourage you to commit to them, no matter what. Unless the house is burning down, they happen! An excellent way to stay on track is to set up a support group or find a buddy and hold each other accountable in your self-care practices.

If simply hearing the news of the day affects your ability to think, cope, or function well, it may be wise to stop and evaluate your self-care. Your resistance or engagement with political news does not have to be an all-or-nothing proposition—stay engaged or completely check out. You can make choices and learn tactics to process information in a way that works for you.

## What Exactly Is Self-Care?

Mary McCoy, a licensed social worker, writes in *Money Crashers:* "Self-care is a very active and powerful choice to engage in the activities that are required to gain or maintain an optimal level of overall health. And in this case, overall health includes not just the physical, but the psychological, emotional, social, and spiritual components of an individual's well-being." When you are spending energy on political or social action, nourishing your mind, body, and spirit is of the utmost importance. Consciously developing a mindful strategy for your activism is a form of self-care. How you deal with the news of the day or where you focus your time and energy is all related to self-care. It may be as simple as deciding to watch the news earlier in the day if watching it right before bed causes you to have difficulty sleeping. If you spend countless hours mulling over your fears and concerns, choose to take a break and have some fun. This is neither self-indulgent nor letting the resistance down. It is worthwhile and necessary.

Unfortunately, when most of us are pressed for time, self-care becomes one of the first things to fall by the wayside. It is precisely at these times that self-care should be most steadfastly adhered to! It is the oil in your engine; without it, you will be functioning at less than full power and after a while, burn out. It is, yet again, another aspect of integrity.

Kathy is a committed refugee activist. She is often asked how she deals with the magnitude of the unending suffering. Her answer: "I focus on the person right in front of me to make a chaotic situation manageable, and I also make sure I take good care of myself. When

I am overwhelmed, I take a break and remind myself that it is for the good of all if I am in good shape."

While volunteering at a refugee camp in Greece, Kathy both witnessed and experienced firsthand the importance of responsible self-care and how it affects not just the individuals who are out of integrity with themselves, but also everyone around them. The majority of refugees arriving from Syria on overcrowded and flimsy dinghies on the shores of the Greek island of Lesvos are soaking wet. In the winter months, this can be life-threatening. It is critical to get them into dry clothes quickly, but this involves them lining up wet, in freezing temperatures, and waiting their turn. When it is time, they go into a tent where volunteers assess their size and needs. If some of their clothing is not wet, they do not get a replacement; they must turn in all wet clothes for recycling. A marvelous group of women calling themselves "Dirty Girls of Lesvos" made it their mission to launder the wet clothes for reuse. Before that, the wet clothes were thrown away. The Dirty Girls are an inspiring and powerful example of volunteerism and activism that began with two women simply picking up trash and doing some laundry. Helping the men, women, and children into dry clothes is a chaotic and time-consuming process. There are language barriers and other challenges, and all the while, many others wait in line, literally freezing. It is highly stressful for everyone.

On one occasion, a volunteer was screaming at the women and children she was working with. These are traumatized people who have fled war, bombing, death, torture, the abuse of smugglers, and more, and taken a harrowing journey to reach Lesvos. This volunteer had been working too long and too hard, and the pressure was obviously getting to her. "I am sure she had the best of intentions initially, but by not taking care of her own needs, she had reached a breaking point and had a damaging effect on the refugees as well as the volunteers who were trying to handle an impossibly trying situation. We were forced to focus our attention and precious energy on this woman rather than on those in such desperate need. It caused a great deal of stress and impacted our ability to do what we needed to do," remembers Kathy. This may be an extreme example, but it clearly demonstrates the need for each person to take responsibility for their own proper self-care in order to be part of the solution, not the problem.

Self-care is another one of those simple concepts with which it is not always easy to follow through. You may hold a shadow belief that self-care is indulgent or a sign of weakness, which inhibits you from making it a priority. But the impact of unchecked overwhelm and stress—as well as other emotions—can be costly. According to the Mayo Clinic, one of the country's leading research hospitals, stress can have a serious affect your body, thoughts, and feelings, as well as your behavior. Stress that's left unchecked and neglect of yourself can manifest in a multitude of ways.

Common effects of stress on the body include:

- Headache
- Fogginess
- Muscle tension or pain

- Chest pain
- Fatigue
- Stomach upset
- Palpitations
- Decrease in sex drive
- Digestive issues
- Sleep problems
- Inflammation and joint pain
- High blood pressure
- High cholesterol
- Weight gain or loss
- Hair loss

Stress also affects mood, leading to:

- Anxiety
- Confusion
- Anger
- Restlessness
- Lack of motivation or focus

- Feeling overwhelmed
- Irritability
- Sadness or depression
- Loss of connection with self or others
- Diminishment or loss of optimism, compassion, faith, love, or hope

And common effects of stress on behavior are:

- Overeating or undereating
- Tantrums and outbursts
- Drug or alcohol abuse
- Tobacco use
- Social withdrawal
- Lack of exercise
- Shopping addiction

## Put Your Oxygen Mask On First

Most of us are familiar with this ubiquitous announcement made by flight attendants prior to takeoff. In simple terms, you are told that if you aren't breathing, you are of no use to anyone! While a total lack of oxygen is a rare occurrence, the intention here can be applied throughout our lives. If you are not taking care of yourself, you will not have the resources to continue effective work in your resistance or life.

It's easy to negate the importance of taking care of ourselves, especially when we work to effect change or help others. It often seems easier to put our needs on the back burner and prioritize everyone and everything else beyond ourselves. This is a mistake and a costly one for all involved. If you are not functioning at your optimal level, whom are you helping? Are you actually advancing the goal you are working toward? If you're running on empty or burnt out, you will be of no help to anyone and may even drain valuable resources needed elsewhere. The volunteer in Greece is the perfect example. And we're betting you don't want to be *that* person.

You may be thinking, "What are you talking about…take care of myself? I can barely deal with what I have on my plate and you want me to do more?" We get it. Fair enough. However, it's at times of overwhelm that your self-care is more important than ever. If you're going to sacrifice your well-being, you cannot possibly be at your best, save the world, and take care of your loved ones and yourself. None of us can do it all.

## Self-Care Is Not Selfish (Lose the Guilt!)

Perhaps you were taught from a very young age that putting your needs first was selfish. You may have had role models who showed you how selfless they were by never taking care of themselves, constantly working (workaholics), sacrificing their needs for others (people pleasers), or being the martyr. Or perhaps you were told that you were lazy or self-indulgent if you chose to take care of yourself. Maybe you come from a religious tradition that preaches sacrifice and selflessness. Women, in particular, are shown and taught by society, their families, and the media that they should be able to do it all and keep a smile on their faces. However, we cannot rely on others to look out for our well-being because no one is coming to rescue us. The responsibility is solely ours. This fact was a life-altering concept for us both.

In his 2016 book, *At Home in the World*, Zen master Thich Nhat Hanh, who has been a social and environmental activist for more than forty years, writes that, "[I]f we don't maintain a balance between our work and the nourishment we need, we won't be very successful. The practice of walking meditation, mindful breathing, allowing our body and mind to rest, and getting in touch with the refreshing and healing elements inside and around us is crucial for our survival."

Nhat Hanh also suggests that in the face of aggression or discrimination, it can be helpful to first sit and find your center, rather than react to events. "Non-action sometimes is very powerful," he has said about activism. "Sometimes we underestimate someone sitting very calm, very solid and not reacting and that they can touch a place of peace, a place of love, a place of nondiscrimination. That is not inaction."

Dan Harris, *Nightline* anchor and author of *Meditation for Fidgety Skeptics*, toured the United States on his "10% Happier" meditation tour. In Tempe, Arizona, Harris came across Sargeant Raj Johnson of the Tempe police force, who expressed the fear that if he got too happy, he'd lose his edge. However, Sargent Johnson's entire department engaged in a meditation program and afterward found that they were *more* effective—in dealing with tense situations, in their performance, in being able to communicate and calm heightened situations, as well as in gaining the trust of citizens.

## Self-Care: It's Your Choice

The choices we make every day, even the small ones, are more important than we may realize. Who we are is a direct result of the decisions and choices we've made in our lives—both negative and positive. Giovanni, a lonely single man in his forties, lacked self-confidence around others and often chose to isolate himself. Many times, Giovanni declined social invitations in favor of curling up on the couch with his dog. He did this to minimize his social discomfort but found that he was alone and lonely. The choices Giovanni made led him to an undesirable outcome in his life.

Eleanor dreamed of being a doctor for as long as she could remember. Like all of us, she often faced choices that would either lead her toward her dream or sabotage it. Eleanor was not perfect in every decision but generally stayed the course and made choices that would forward her dream. On many occasions, she stayed home to study rather than go to a party, dinner, or movie. Today Eleanor is the head of her department at a prestigious hospital. She turned her dream into reality through the choices she made along the way.

Usually, there is some underlying component in our disempowering choices. In other words, we are getting something out of them.

Going back once again to our favorite news-watching example, you may want to experience less angst about everything that is happening politically yet find yourself consuming copious amounts of negative news. You might want to be known as a well-informed citizen, maybe even the go-to person for the day's news, but the reality is, this need is causing you more harm than good. Another example of this concept is the resistor who is subconsciously attached to being seen as a self-sacrificing martyr for the cause. Neglecting self-care fulfills her need to be perceived in this way. However, she is often sick and exhausted and not able to contribute as much as she would like. In addition, she often complains to other volunteers, taking up their precious time and energy.

Like the self-sacrificing martyr or the well-informed citizen, do you have an underlying need that is somehow being met by denying yourself proper self-care? What are you getting out of not taking care of yourself? When you have your answer, take a moment to explore whether this perceived benefit is worth the cost. We believe it is not and that a self-care plan should be a priority for everyone.

## Self-Care Starter Kit

*Real self-care brings self-awareness —
it is not the same as narcissism or selfishness which
are the effect of a lack of self-awareness.*
—Gail Stearns, Dean of the Wallace All Faiths
Chapel and Associate Professor of
Religious Studies, Chapman University

"Most people understand that stress is more manageable when they're feeling happy, healthy, loved, and at peace," says Mary McCoy. A major component of self-care is making choices that nurture the emotions you wish to cultivate. Asking yourself what practices contribute to these states of mind is the start of an effective self-care plan.

Any number of pathways to self-care are found in the emotional, physical, and spiritual realms. Some may involve letting go: sugar, smoking, negative people. Some may involve adding more: exercise, time with friends, meditation, things that bring you joy, doing nothing at all. Self-care is a highly personal endeavor. It is important to choose elements that truly speak to you, not simply those things you think you "should" do because they are the trend of the moment. Paying attention to your needs and desires is a critical aspect of self-care—a form of integrity. Trusting yourself, wherever you are at any given moment, is a great start.

Before deciding on your self-care practices, take an honest look at yourself. Where are you out of personal integrity? Are you carrying tension in your body from the anger you feel toward Trump and his supporters? Are you waking up with headaches from fear or trepidation about what you may hear from the administration? Are you yelling at your kids or partner because yelling at the TV doesn't work? Are you looking around and thinking everyone is an idiot? These are all clues that will help you pinpoint where you are out of integrity and where self-care may be lacking.

The next step involves considering choices you can make that will eliminate or decrease your stress. This phase is not always easy because it may require you to disappoint others or even yourself should you decide to let go of something that matters to you but isn't a top priority. Another challenge might be that you have taken on too much and ignored your well-being because you have believed that you are a good person if you neglect yourself, put others' needs first, or always say yes—and you are not a good person if you don't. But we want to take a moment to remind you that you must put your oxygen mask on before helping others if you are committed to finding balance in your life.

Cheryl Richardson, in her book *The Art of Extreme Self-Care*, writes: "The art of extreme self-care takes patience, commitment, and practice. It initially requires a willingness to sit with some pretty uncomfortable feelings, too, such as guilt—for putting your needs first, fear—of being judged and criticized by others, or anxiety—from challenging long-held beliefs and behaviors. It's an organic, evolutionary process; an art as opposed to a science."

Kathy recognized that she was overwhelmed and out of personal integrity. A major source of anxiety and overwhelm was the many emails and notifications with alarmist headlines that she received daily. "I realized that simply reading the subject lines created an insidious underlying anxiety that was hard to shake. After recognizing this, I made a conscious choice to review where my emails came from, choose the most valuable to me, and unsubscribe from the rest. I felt an immediate sense of relief." Kathy's experience is not unique. Taking care of yourself and making choices with your well-being in mind is empowering. It's not always easy, but it's always worth it.

## Time: Your Most Precious Resource

*It's really clear that the most precious resource we all have is time.*
—Steve Jobs, inventor and entrepreneur

It's easy to take time for granted. We waste it by acting as if it is unlimited—but it's not. Choices you make surrounding your time may seem inconsequential in the moment but will determine where you find yourself in the years ahead.

If we all have the same twenty-four hours to spend each day, why does it seem some people are so much more productive than others? The answer is that they are selective with their time and make conscious choices about how they spend it.

When you start treating your time as your most valuable resource, both enjoying and respecting it, you will protect it as the gift that it is.

## Getting Clear on Your Priorities and Time Management

Many of our clients are shocked by what they find when they put the use of their time down on paper. They are surprised to see how much time they waste on things that are not important to them and how little time they actually devote to what matters most. To determine whether you are spending your time on what matters most to you, make a list of everything begging for your attention (family, career, activism, self-care, relationships, home obligations, etc.). After each item, attach a percentage reflecting the average weekly time you spend on that particular item. Your total should add up to 100 percent. Don't worry about figuring out exact percentages; simply close your eyes and allow a number to pop into your consciousness for each item. When you have gone through the list, make adjustments that feel right to reach 100 percent.

Create a second list with the same initial categories but reorganize and prioritize your list according to the percentage of time you would like to devote to each. Again, get quiet, take a few breaths, and let the answers present themselves. Is there anything you'd like to be doing that was not on the original list? Add it and then note the percentage of your time you would like to devote to this. Your total should again add up to 100 percent.

Donna was on the committee for her local People's Climate March, where she met Sam. He shared with her how stressed he was by the many things demanding his attention. He had been overwhelmed with commitments prior to the election but now, upon adding resistance to his plate, he was unravelling. Without a clear understanding of his priorities to guide him in setting goals and boundaries, he felt that he was in the eye of a hurricane. Donna directed Sam to begin the process of prioritizing by creating his lists. This is what he came back with:

Sam's current time expenditure:
Family–10%
Career–60%
Relationships–5%
Activism–22%

Chores (shopping, laundry, cleaning, repairs, yard work, screen time, etc.)–3%

Self-care (artistic endeavors, meditating, journaling, exercising, travel)–0%

Sam's ideal time expenditure:
Family–25%
Career–40%
Relationships–10%
Activism–10%
Chores–5%
Self-care–10%

Sam now has the necessary information to make adjustments and bring himself into integrity. He recognizes that he spends more time at work than he would like or is necessary. He wants to invest less time on home obligations and more on family, relationships, and activism. Most importantly, Sam notices a glaring omission. He has not been incorporating any meaningful self-care into his life and now commits to including it in his weekly routine.

After completing both lists, take time to evaluate them. How do your lists compare? Are there any surprises? Are any items listed because of a sense of obligation or some reason other than that they are a priority for you? Cross them off the list! Of course, work may seem more like an obligation than a priority, but we can all probably agree that eating and paying rent are priorities and therefore, so is work!

Where does self-care fall on your list? Have you made it a priority? Do you need to adjust the time you devote to self-care? Now that you have clarified the time you will spend, let's turn to specifying how you will use that time.

Donna's self-care exploration led her to practice organization as an act of self-care. "Disorganization was causing me a lot of overwhelm and frustration. Spending a little time and effort to organize my priorities and my desk made all the difference and helped me become more productive in my activism." Donna used the Targeted Area of Activism exercise (see Chapter 5) to clarify that the environment was the issue most important to her and set the goal of sending five environmentally focused postcards each day to targeted officials. "I felt that I couldn't keep up with it—it was almost crazy-making! I decided to purchase, pre-address, and stamp a stack of postcards (I even made it fun with different colors—hot pink, lime green, bright orange) to be readily available each day. Now, every morning, I can easily write my five cards without needing to scramble for the cards, postage, and addresses. And whenever something comes up that I want to respond to, I simply grab a card and write a short note expressing my opposition to some crazy situation, policy, nomination, or bill, or my gratitude or support for a positive vote or position." She continues: "As a result of getting more organized, I am more effective and feel a sense of pride and peacefulness knowing that I'm doing my part."

## The Bottom Line

Self-care is life-preserving and life-sustaining. It is a way to invest in yourself, your loved ones, your community, and the world. More than a luxury, self-care is a responsibility we have to ourselves and others. It strengthens our ability to cope with the mind-numbing political events of each day, supports us in our activism, and allows us to create more of what we want in our lives. Practing self-care also gives others permission to do the same for themselves. There is no day more perfect than today to (re)-commit yourself to self-care.

CHAPTER 5

# Ready, Set, Go!

*I feel the injustice in the world and use it as a catalyst. To stand up and make a difference, to have my voice heard.*
—Diane Altomare, author and life coach

Taking action is a powerful way to channel emotions and hold feelings of negativity and powerlessness at bay. Lynne Twist, activist and founder of The Hunger Project and Pachamama Alliance, writes, "The negativity that surrounds so many of us with regard to our political climate is valid, but I have realized that it makes no difference. In fact, it makes a negative difference. What allows you to get out of the doldrums, the depression, the upset, the anger, the resentment about the way that the country is headed, is to get in action. When you're in action, all of those feelings will go away."

Panic-stricken hysteria only serves to keep us focused on what's wrong, allowing neither progress nor positive change. The key is turning panic into action. Instead of suffering with our "hair on fire," can we mindfully determine which issues most concern us and take empowered action on them? Emotional upheaval, while a great motivator, is unsustainable and will slow us down and lessen our collective impact. Perhaps it behooves all of us to ignore the tweets and place our energy on getting involved on local, national, or international levels, wherever we can best make a difference. But how we proceed matters because, as we hope you now understand, there are costs to not paying attention and falling into an integrity lapse.

"Activist" is a label that you may find intimidating. Perhaps the little nay-saying shadow voice in your head whispers, "Who am I to think I can be an activist?" or "*Real* activists are (fill in the blank) and I'm not like that." But if you are distraught and frustrated by this administration's disregard for the environment, the health care of millions, and immigrants, or appalled by its misogyny, homophobia, and racism—honestly, the list is too long to complete—it may be a sign that you are ready to step up. And once you take any action, large or small, you *are* an activist.

Donna's late friend John Denver told her, concerning the plight of the environment, "You don't have to do it all but there is *something* you can do—it can be easy and doesn't have to be a great sacrifice. If it comes out of your heart and spirit and inclinations, that's the easy thing! Do what you can do as an expression of who you are and an expression of your relationship to nature and the environment. You do the thing you can do, I'll do the thing I can do, and we'll inspire others to do what they can do."

Whether you are just beginning, have been resisting since Trump's election, or are a lifetime activist, it is important to stop, connect within, take stock, and clarify your priorities. In this chapter, you will identify the primary target area of your activism and where you will focus the bulk of your time and attention. You will get clear on your expansive vision, the ideal vision you hold for your target area, because it is the surest way to set yourself up for success. When you do not have a clear vision and do not take the time to set goals—a series of smaller specific steps or objectives to get you there—you risk never bringing your vision to fruition. Without a clear expansive vision and set of goals for achieving it, you will most likely spin your wheels, waste time, and soon become frustrated and unproductive. You may find yourself working twice as hard and half as effectively, and end up burned out. Have you heard the well-known phrase, "If you fail to plan, you plan to fail"? It's difficult to experience a sense of accomplishment when you are unclear what the goal is. It's no fun to run around in circles, but that is probably what you will do if you fail to clearly define, formulate, and implement a goal-oriented action plan to bring your expansive vision to reality. This holds true not only for your activism but for everything else you'd like to achieve in life. Without a vision and a plan to support it, you may stumble upon a positive outcome, but it will be by chance. Think about it: do you really want to leave the future of your country, not to mention your personal dreams and goals, to chance?

To feel productive, avoid wheel-spinning and overwhelm, and keep from leaving your role as a resister (and human being) to chance, you will want to make mindful choices, because time is a finite resource. We guide and support our clients to clarify what's most important to them and to use their time in a manner that aligns with their vision and goals. By defining what matters most to you and where you want to have the most impact, and by making time-management decisions accordingly, you create a greater chance for success, achieve a sense of accomplishment and productivity, and finally put an end to the old hamster-on-a-wheel routine!

In this dire political environment, we have no time to waste, no one to spare. You matter, your passion matters, your creativity matters, and your time matters. You need to shine and be the fundraising, polling-place-coordinating, phone-bank-volunteering, petition-signing, protest-marching resistor that you are!

Clarifying your goals and creating plans of action will get you there, as well as everywhere else you want to go.

## Your Targeted Area of Activism

We are all pulled in multiple directions each day. We take on more and more and think we are getting more done, but what if we told you that you may be more effective doing less? You, most likely, must still manage your personal and work responsibilities but are now also bombarded by nonstop political chaos. Each day we think what we hear about this administration and Republican-run Congress couldn't possibly get any worse, and yet we wake up to find that indeed it has. Everything feels urgent, and it is easy to fall into an I-need-to-do-it-all-now mindset. But it bears repeating that this is not an efficient way of managing your activism (or life) and will probably lead to burnout and other undesirable consequences. It may affect your relationships at home or at work, or even your health.

As much as we'd all like to think we are superhuman, individually we can't do it all. What would it take for you to know and believe that you cannot be responsible for everyone or everything, and trust that others are as committed as you and will step in and pick up the slack? You may be thinking, "But there are so many things I want to do!" There may be more than one issue that is important to you, but spreading yourself too thin is more like dabbling, lessening your effectiveness in all areas. There is nothing wrong with dabbling if that is your choice, but it should be a conscious choice, not one made by default. By focusing on one targeted area for your activism, you can become a force. Rest assured, those with the most passion will step in to take action in the areas that are priorities for them. This is not to suggest you should not make your calls, sign petitions, or send postcards, but rather to hone in on where you will focus the bulk of your time and attention.

What is the area in which you want to become educated, understand the nuances, and be able to dialogue effectively and educate others? If we each focus our energy and creativity on our top priority, we will all be at our most committed and passionate and become more powerful as a whole. You cannot do it all by yourself, but together we can! And doesn't that seem like more fun?

## Let's Get Specific

You may be clear about which area you want to focus on and what is most critical for you, or you may find yourself struggling to narrow it down. Neither of these is right or wrong; they are simply descriptions of where you are at this moment. If you are ready to get clear on what matters most to you, the Resistance Wheel below will help. If you already know, it's still an eye-opening exercise!

BEYOND RESISTANCE

## RESISTANCE WHEEL

- Health Care
- Civil Rights and Social Justice
- Environment
- Immigration and Refugees
- Women's Issues
- Local, State, and Federal Elections
- Education

Each segment of the Resistance Wheel represents one of the major areas where there is resistance to Trump's agenda. This is by no means an exhaustive list but merely some of the larger issues. Feel free to add your own category if we have left out something that is important to you. We have left a blank space for this purpose.

Review the wheel and observe your reactions. Jot down some notes if you choose. When ready, take yourself through the process below in order to pinpoint your major area of concern and commitment. For those who already have a clear targeted area, this process will serve to solidify that choice—or perhaps you will be in for a surprise!

Before you begin, remember that it is important to trust yourself and what you hear from within throughout the process. Use your breath as a mechanism to connect deeply with yourself and your inner wisdom. If you begin to experience doubt or are afraid of choosing the "wrong" category, gently remind yourself, without judgment, that there is no right or wrong answer. Doubt is simply fear popping up, trying to protect you from some undefined bogeyman, such as making a mistake. Hold the intention to trust yourself and the process.

## Targeted Area of Activism Process

Have a pen and paper handy and find a quiet space where you won't be distracted. Affirm your trust in your inner voice and remember to use your breath. You will find a recorded version of this process on our website: *www.beyondresistancebook.com*.

- Gently close your eyes, breathe, relax, feel yourself in your chair, and consciously choose to let go of anything standing between you and being present to this exercise. Affirm that there are no right or wrong answers to the following questions and that you will trust whatever you hear from within without judgment. Follow your breath and allow yourself to go within and connect to that place of knowledge and insight. . .the place where truth resides.

- Begin to bring your desire to be an agent of change into your consciousness. Continue to center your attention on your breath as you think about the Resistance Wheel. You are going to simply dwell in each category for a moment as you listen on the deepest level and observe how you are impacted as each category is spoken aloud. Notice what happens within your body. Do you feel neutral or only slightly affected? Or are you deeply moved, experiencing an intense response or tension in one particular area of your body? Perhaps there is a tightening in your chest or you want to cry or scream. Do you sense anger rising? Notice your responses as we continue through each area of the wheel and jot your observations down as we go.

- Let's begin with **Education**. Breathe and let your mind and heart float around the topic of education. Focus on the education policies you see being put into place and the appointees leading our country's education policy. As you do this, pay attention to your feelings and reactions. Are you noticing anything significant? Are your muscles tensing? Is your breath changing? Do you observe anything else that seems significant? When you are ready, jot down a few notes describing your response to this topic.

- Take another deep breath and consider **Health Care**. Center your attention on the attempts to repeal and replace the Affordable Care Act and the impact that losing it will have on millions of people. Notice your physical and emotional reactions to this. Are you disturbed, but a little removed, or does it infuriate you? Do you feel a tightening in your jaw? Take some brief notes, remembering to stay in the process.

- Now move on to **Civil Rights and Social Justice**. This category includes racism, ageism, labor policy, criminal justice, and related issues. How do you feel when you let thoughts of how this administration is handling civil rights wash over you? Are you motivated to act? Do you feel touched on the deepest levels? Jot down anything of significance that arises.

- Breathe deeply and bring your attention to the **Environment**. How do you feel when you think about the United States pulling out of the Paris Climate Agreement? What is your reaction to what is being done to the Environmental Protection Agency, and the abolishment of laws protecting the environment? Is this the most critical subject that requires your attention? Does the idea of being a part of the movement to protect the environment inspire you? Take some brief notes.

- Focus now on **Immigration**. Think about the travel ban; the effort to round up and deport millions of people, separating families; the Immigration & Customs Enforcement (ICE) raids; the repeal of the Deferred Action for Childhood Arrivals policy (DACA), building a wall on our country's southern border. Is this what you feel most passionate about? Take some notes.

- Now, turn your attention to **Women's Issues**. What comes up for you when you immerse yourself in the multiple issues impacting women: health care, violence, sexual harassment, reproductive rights, and job and wage inequality? Do these issues touch you on the deepest levels? Do they inspire you to prioritize taking action in this area? Jot down some brief thoughts.

- Take another deep breath and bring upcoming **Local, State, and Federal Elections** into your awareness. Does the importance of winning seats inspire you to support candidates' campaigns with your time or money, educate and raise awareness of candidates and issues, or help with getting out the vote? What are the feelings that arise when you think about the importance of future elections?

- Finally, take a moment to bring to mind any area that is important to you that we have not touched upon. Allow yourself to connect with this area and notice your thoughts and feelings. When you are ready, take some notes.
- Now that you've gone through each area on the Resistance Wheel, ask yourself which is most critical to you? Where did you experience the biggest response and feel most moved? Where do you most need to focus your attention and work for change? Was it the environment? Women's issues? Elections? (Note: If you heard more than one answer, name them again, and ask yourself, "In which of these areas do I most need to focus my attention?") Trust whatever you hear without questioning it. Write down your answer.
- Before you complete this process, check back in with yourself and ask your inner wisdom if there is anything else it wants you to know. Stay with your breath for a moment and wait to see if anything comes up. If so, write it down.
- When you feel that you have received all that you need from this exercise, take a moment to acknowledge yourself for the work you have done. Affirm your trust in your inner wisdom and your desire to act upon it. And then, when you are ready, open your eyes and reconnect with your surroundings.

Fantastic! Hopefully you have discovered or affirmed which topic matters most to you. If you have not, take a break and come back to the process when you feel fresh and ready to try again. Remember not to judge or put pressure on yourself if you are having difficulty—it will only keep you from the answers you seek.

## Your Expansive Vision

Now that you have chosen your targeted area of activism, it is time to clarify your expansive vision. An expansive vision is a broad reflection of your deepest desires. It should inspire you, provide purpose to your activism, and serve as a north star, a compass point to guide your choices and actions. The word "vision" comes from the Latin *visionem*, meaning wisdom. It follows, then, that holding a vision is having the wisdom to see beyond current events in expectation of a greater result.

Sometimes it can be difficult to put your expansive vision into words because you are describing something that doesn't exist yet. As you become more trusting of your inner voice, it will be easier to connect with your priorities. In calling forth your vision, don't settle for what you know is possible—dream big! Embracing ideals that seem "unrealistic" is part of what it means to engage in social and political activism. Everybody has a unique contribution to make to the resistance effort, no matter how big or small. Yours will become evident as you step into targeted action.

Many of us have the tendency to think and talk about what we *don't* want—both in life and in our activism. This is a particularly easy habit to fall into in this political environment. When you develop your expansive vision, it is important to frame it in terms of what you stand for, not what you are against.

Susan and Rebecca, both friends of Donna, created expansive visions. Susan determined that her targeted area of activism is the environment and describes her expansive vision as follows: "I see us all living sustainably. I see a thriving planet where every sentient being has clean air to breathe and fresh water to drink. I see us all with access to healthy, non-toxic, unprocessed food that nourishes us. I see climate change taken seriously by our politicians, and laws and regulations reflecting that priority."

Rebecca describes her ideal vision in the area of women's issues as follows: "I see a world where there is gender equality, where women receive the same pay and opportunities as men. I see women around the world enjoying the same rights as men in general. I see a world where little girls are taught that they are much more than what they look like and where all women have the right to make decisions about their own lives and bodies."

Both Susan and Rebecca have successfully articulated their visions by dwelling in the possibility of a future that inspires them. They have draped their visions around themselves like superheroes' capes to propel them forward into positive action.

Now it's time for you to become clear on *your* expansive vision.

## Expansive Vision Process

Have your pen and paper handy and find a quiet space in your home or garden. Make sure you are somewhere you feel nurtured and secure and you won't be distracted. If you begin to doubt yourself or even judge this exercise to be a waste of time, simply reaffirm your trust in your inner voice and the process. You will

*Ready, Set, Go!*

find a recorded version of this process on our website: *www.beyondresistancebook.com*.

• Let your eyes close gently and allow yourself to be curious about what might be possible in the future. Pause for these next few moments to be in the stillness, connecting with your inner wisdom. If your mind drifts away, gently pause, without self-judgment, and bring yourself back to the rhythm and sound of your breath. As you inhale, take in all the love that's available to you. And as you exhale, allow a sense of ease to surround you.

• Acknowledge the calmness, like the surface of a glassy lake, gently centering, allowing the silence to guide you. There's nothing you need to do but be present in this moment. Notice any negative thoughts that come up, acknowledge them, and simply return to your breath once again.

• As you continue to breathe easily with an open heart, spend a few moments reflecting on what is most important to you. Stand firmly in this place of wisdom and clarity and ask, "What is the most inspired vision I hold for [insert your targeted area of activism]? What would this look like in a perfect world?

• Allow your mind to open, trusting that there are no right or wrong answers. Let your expansive vision effortlessly appear from a place deep within, knowing that if you can see it, it is possible.

• Take your time as you allow the details of your vision to become more and more clear. Listen for the information that is coming to you. Open space within for the fullness of your vision to emerge and express itself—it may be specific or more general, either is okay. Receive the information with gratitude and give yourself the time to allow all to be revealed. Take brief notes as you go along but remember to stay in your process.

- Ask yourself if there is anything more that your inner wisdom wants to share with you. If there is nothing further, take a moment to thank your inner voice for guiding you and acknowledge yourself for the work you have done. Then open your eyes and come back to the room. Allow yourself a few moments to write down the details of your expanded vision.

Well done! You have developed a clear, expansive vision, one that will serve as a powerful tool if you commit to action and allow it to be your guiding force. You can weigh each choice and action against whether it will lead you closer to the realization of your vision or farther away from it. For example, if your expansive vision is a world that produces 50 percent less plastic, will buying a plastic bottle of water lead you closer to or farther from your vision? Keep your vision in mind every day. Write it down and post it where you can see it to stay connected to what matters most to you. Set the intention to be an inspired catalyst for change.

## A Tip: Vision Boards

Vision boards have been around for a long time. We continue to use them ourselves and believe they are an invaluable tool. A vision board is a reminder of our priorities. It helps us clarify our goals and dreams and remain focused and inspired to make choices in alignment with them. It is not simply an expression of a desire for a particular end result; it is a resource to motivate us. The reality that we create is a direct reflection of where we focus our energy and atten-

*Ready, Set, Go!*

tion. When we spend a few minutes with our board each day, we build momentum toward the fulfillment of our vision. It's easy to lose sight of dreams and goals when you don't remember what they are. Keep your board front and center so that you are reminded daily to honor your vision. You may even choose to say a positive affirmation asking to be a vehicle for its manifestation.

You might wish to create a sacred space in which to put your board together by lighting a candle and playing some inspiring music. Or, you may want to invite a group of supportive friends to create together. One of the easiest ways to create a vision board is to use a cork, magnetic, or poster board upon which you can glue or pin images and words you find in magazines or elsewhere that inspire you or represent feelings you'd like to enhance or create. Gather some magazines or other materials, scissors, and whatever else you might need to create your board. Connect with your expansive vision and begin to add images and words to your board until you see your vision come to life. Looking at your board should feel uplifting and leave you infused with possibility, creativity, and inspiration! Keep in mind that your vision "reminders" don't need to be limited to a vision board. Be creative. Think of ways to keep your vision front and center. One of Kathy's favorite techniques is putting a colored string around her wrist. Donna likes to put sticky note reminders on her bathroom mirror. Whatever works for you is a perfect idea!

## Turning Your Vision into Reality

The most powerful way to turn your expansive vision into reality is to identify steps and benchmarks to guide you on your journey. Think of these as milestones that will lead toward the fulfillment of your vision.

Your expansive vision will keep you engaged and committed for the long-term, it is also the key to identifying specific goals to get you there. They work together: your vision guides the identification of your goals, and the completion of these goals supports the realization of your vision. If you consider your vision as a blueprint and your goals as the tools and building materials, you will be on your way in no time.

## Without a Goal, How Can You Score a Touchdown?

*The trouble with not having a goal is that you can spend your life running up and down the field and never score.*
—William (Bill) Copeland, American poet, writer, and historian

Setting goals involves clarifying the specific path you will take to bring your vision to life. When you become immersed in negative feelings about the news of the day, week, or month, it can be difficult to think or have clarity about what you need to do, but with a previously thought-out goal and plan of action, you can immediately step into action without needing to figure it out. This can be a godsend when you feel overwhelmed.

Think of a goal as having a tangible and measurable end result. It is an action or project to be achieved within a more-or-less fixed time frame that leads you toward your expansive vision. Setting goals will help clarify your thoughts and ideas, focus your efforts to save precious time, and use your resources productively. When you think of it in these terms, a goal becomes a joy to work on.

There several important guidelines that are critical to follow when establishing your goal. They each focus on keeping your goal clear and actionable. George T. Doran, consultant and former director of corporate planning for Washington Water Power Company, invented the acronym SMART to help you remember the five "golden rules of goal setting." The SMART system helps you set goals with confidence and enjoy the satisfaction that comes with knowing you achieved what you set out to do. It feels great to accomplish a goal, and that satisfaction will spur you on to continue forward. We modified the acronym slightly by adding Inspirational and Emotional, to give you an even greater advantage. Here are the *Beyond Resistance*-endorsed SMARTIE goals:

**S-Specific**

What do I want to accomplish?

Why is this goal important?

Who is involved?

Which resources or limitations are involved?

**M-Measurable**

How much?

How many?

How will I know when I've accomplished my goal?

Setting a clear marker for success is a critical part of the process and makes it harder to ignore your achievements. If you are someone who falls into the "I didn't do enough" mindset (most people are) and your goals or action steps are not defined in a clear and detailed manner, you may neglect to acknowledge your accomplishments.

### A-Attainable

How realistic is your goal?

Is it a goal that is not wholly dependent on an act of God or another person?

Do you have the resources to devote to accomplishing your goal?

Don't mistake this with thinking outside the box in your expansive vision. Your goal should be challenging yet achievable.

### R-Relevant

Does this seem worth my time and effort?

Is this the right time to work on this goal?

Is this goal in alignment with my other efforts and needs?

### T-Time-bound

By when will I complete this goal?

What can I do six months from now to complete this goal?

What can I do six weeks from now?

What can I do today?

### I-Inspirational

Does this goal give me goosebumps? Am I uplifted, energized, excited?

Is there something I need to modify to truly be inspired?

If it doesn't move you, it's unlikely that you will be motivated to take action.

### E-Emotional

Describe the emotions you will experience upon the completion of your goal. State these in the present tense, as if they have already occurred ("I feel fulfilled" as opposed to "I will feel fulfilled").

Use these emotions as motivators while working toward your goal.

You will identify your goal from a heart-centered place as you did when homing in on a targeted area of activism and clarifying an expansive vision. Bring your talents and joy to the table. We ask you to consider several questions before beginning the process of determining your goal.

## Goal-Setting Journaling Exercise

- What do you most enjoy doing?
- What do you least enjoy doing?
- What are you good at? Are you a writer? Would you enjoy writing letters to the editor? Articles or op-eds? Is motivational or public speaking your strength? Do you think you would make a great elected official? Can you envision yourself running for public office? Are you an educator? A protester? A great organizer? Can you plan a fundraising event, protest, or march? Do you enjoy hosting and see yourself hosting a house party or watch party for a film or television show like Van Jones's *The Messy Truth* on CNN? Are you a talented communicator? Are you good on the phone? Do you simply enjoy talking with people?
- How much time can you reasonably commit per day or week without overcommitting?

When thinking about your goal, don't settle for what seems like a no-brainer—because this is likely to be the lowest rung of your "potential ladder." Open yourself up to possibility, even if it's intimidating. Many of us are afraid to reach because we are afraid to fail, but we should remember that many of the greatest achievements in the world were only achieved after countless failures.

Don't let fear or defeat stand in the way of your shining at your brightest. You cheat yourself and the rest of the world when you don't step out of your comfort zone. Choose to feel the discomfort of your fear and do it anyway. Most people who achieve things they are proud of felt fear at some point but pushed through. You will be amazed by who you find yourself becoming!

Another thing: you don't have to reinvent the wheel—unless you want to. Take the time to research groups that are engaged and doing good work in the area you are committing to. Being a part of a community that has a common focus will empower and enrich everyone involved. Indivisible's mission is to fuel a progressive grassroots network to resist the Trump agenda and it is a great place to start. (www.indivisible.org). There are many local chapters that will connect you with resistance members in your community and beyond.

Let's return to Susan and Rebecca for a moment to see what was illuminated for them during the goal-setting process. If you recall, Susan's passion is the environment; she holds a vision that includes sustainable, nontoxic living for all. After getting a better sense of what works best for her from the questions above, Susan determined that to take a fearless step toward her vision, she would work within her community to change 60,000 incandescent light bulbs

*Ready, Set, Go!*

to LED. This was a clear and easily measurable goal that filled her with excitement and purpose in her activism.

Women's issues are most compelling for Rebecca. She envisions a world with gender equality and all that involves. After spending some time reviewing the guideline questions, she dove into the process. Rebecca determined that she wanted to organize three local meetups to write postcards and make calls to representatives in support of Planned Parenthood.

There are no limits to what your goals can be. They can be as simple as writing one postcard a week or as grand as running for public office or working to influence policy. The most important thing to remember is that no goal is too big or too small. If you hear the call and are ready to commit wholeheartedly to taking action, it is a perfect goal.

## Goal-Setting Process

Before we delve further into the goal-setting process, we want to remind you to be gentle with yourself. Give yourself time and space to receive your answers and trust what you hear, even if it does not make sense to you at the moment. Be sure to have a pen and paper handy, and remember, you can find the recorded audio for each of the processes at *www.beyondresistancebook.com*.

• Close your eyes and feel yourself begin to relax wherever you are seated. Notice your breath—the coolness of your inhalation and the release of your exhalation. As you exhale, feel yourself dropping down into a place deep within. It is a protected place where there is no fear, only truth and authenticity. Consciously allow any thoughts that may be present to simply melt away and bring your attention back to your center.

- Allow yourself to visualize all that is going on in your targeted area of activism right now. What is the current situation? Is the administration or Congress trying to make changes or move forward with policies that you don't agree with? Bring these circumstances to mind. What are some of the emotions that come up while you dwell in this space? Take some notes.

- With your next breath, release your hold on these emotions and let them drift away. Allow your expansive vision to come into focus. Step into your magnificent vision and take some time to connect with its details. Fully experience that reality. Remain there for a few moments.

- Take a deep cleansing breath and ask yourself, "What is the first and most important step I need to take to bring my vision to life? What would I do if I knew I couldn't fail?" As you wait for the answer to be revealed, be gentle with yourself. There is no need to put pressure on yourself, either to come up with the perfect response or to hurry. Allow yourself to relax, focus on your breath, and connect with your heart-space. Wait for the answer to appear. Perhaps you are called to run for office, pursue a higher degree, advocate, lobby, or become a local community organizer. Perhaps your goal is to be a watchdog and create a resource for others. Whatever you hear, trust it, even if it seems impossible or ridiculous. When you are clear about the message coming to you, take some brief notes.

- Drop back down inside yourself and take a few moments to imagine having already completed your goal. Connect with the experience and consciously anchor it, and the feelings associated with it, into your body and mind. Take some notes about how it feels to stand in the completion of your goal.

- Now, take a few breaths and visualize yourself beginning the process of bringing your goal to fruition. Ask yourself, "What parts of myself will I need to call upon to achieve my goal?" Perhaps your courageous self? Your relentless self? Your smart self? Wait for your answer and take some notes.

- Holding these qualities in your heart, affirm: "I choose to call upon and nurture my _____ (fill in the blank with the personal trait you identified in the previous step) in order to use it for the greater good. I trust in myself and my inner voice, and I will stand up for what I am called to do." You can repeat this as many times as needed until you have internalized the message.

- Take a moment to acknowledge what you have accomplished during this process. Then, when you are ready, gently open your eyes and come back to the room.

Give yourself some time to take notes or journal about what came up for you. If you had difficulty getting answers, the most critical thing is to treat yourself with kindness. Acknowledge yourself for your efforts, put the exercise aside, and try again when you are ready and relaxed. This process can be used at any time, in any area of your life, with some minor adjustments.

## The Importance of Action Steps

An action step is a concrete measurable action you can take this week (or within any short period of time) to begin the process of reaching your goal. Many people resist being specific while defining their action steps because on some level they don't want to be held responsible or accountable. But as we mentioned above, if your objective is not crystal clear and you are a person who tends to default to the belief that you haven't done enough, you may find yourself back in default mode. A clear objective indicates the unmistakable accomplishment of your goal, with no room for debate. By setting explicit objectives, you take the guesswork out of whether you've done enough.

To begin, take a moment to determine a powerful action step you can perform in the next week that will further your goal. It might be to register yourself as a candidate in the next city council election or to sign up for phone-banking. Be bold; don't simply lapse into something easy, but don't choose something so challenging that failure is likely. Success is important because "success breeds success." Not completing your action step may leave you demoralized, making it more difficult to achieve your goal...and a lot less enjoyable! Find a "buddy" or someone who agrees to support you and hold you accountable to your commitment to complete your goal both thoroughly and on time. Commit to checking in with them at the agreed-upon time and ask them to contact you if they don't hear from you. Whether you have or have not completed what you set out to do, make arrangements for your buddy to talk through with you what your next action step will be. Or recommit to following through on the action.

Rebecca concluded that her first action step would be to design an overall plan for the meetups she wanted to create. She committed to thinking through and researching what would be required and to developing a plan for booking the venue; designing a sign-up sheet for attendees; creating a local representative contact information sheet for easy access; purchasing needed supplies such as pens, stamps, and postcards; and determining whether she would provide refreshments or ask guests to help out. Rebecca asked her friend Jessica to be her buddy and shared her action-step commitment. Knowing she would be held accountable was a powerful motivating force for Rebecca. At the agreed-upon time, Rebecca let Jessica know that she had completed all her tasks. Feeling proud and motivated, she evaluated where she was and determined what her next action step would be. She shared it with Jessica and committed to a completion date, and the process began again.

## Your Resistance Mission Statement

A resistance mission statement is a brief description of what is most important to you, what you want to accomplish, and who you want to be or become in your activism. It is another resource to help focus your energy, actions, behaviors, and decision-making. We are often asked about the difference between a mission statement and an expanded vision. Your expanded vision describes your unique future-based ideal of a particular area. A mission statement is based on the now and defines your priorities and where you will focus your attention. Both serve as guideposts.

While there is no precise formula for creating a resistance mission statement, the following guidelines may be helpful:

- Keep it simple, clear, and brief.

- Think about specific actions, behaviors, habits, and qualities you can bring to the table that will have a significant and positive impact.
- Be sure to frame your statement in positive terms. Describe what you want to do or become, not what you don't. Consider what you stand for, not against. There are always positive alternatives to any negative statements.
- Include character traits and values that you consider particularly important and that you want to develop further — for example, to treat each individual who is homeless with dignity, respect and compassion, or to tackle issues as they arise with integrity and courage.
- Be sure that your statement motivates and inspires so it pulls you forward.

Remember, your mission statement can be fluid and may change as you change and gain new insights and information.

Your statement should guide your day-to-day actions and decision-making. Make it a part of your everyday routine. Post it where you can see and be inspired by it. Kathy's is posted on her bathroom mirror so that she sees it morning and evening while she brushes her teeth. Donna has hers on her vision board.

You can also tailor a mission statement to any other area of your life: your career, relationships, finances, health, etc. Here are a couple of templates that you can use to develop your own mission statements, for your resistance and for any other areas you choose to work on:

"My mission is to (foster a world of harmony and goodwill) by (serving my local community, the environment) through committing to (daily action) in order to (promote positive change, important alliances, and understanding).

"My mission is to (be the change I wish to see in the world) by (being an active voice of tolerance and compassion; living each day with openness, kindness, and gratitude) so that (those qualities will ripple throughout the world; others will feel safe). I will do this by (greeting everyone with a smile, listening, and living my life as a statement of love).

"My mission is to (create a loving, compassionate, and committed intimate relationship with my partner) by (being open-hearted, generous, and honest), so that (I help foster an environment of safety, gratitude, and love). I will do this by (prioritizing the relationship, listening deeply, and supporting my partner in being the best he or she can be).

We went through several iterations of our resistance mission statement during the writing of this book. It evolved as we clarified our goals and purpose, and yours may evolve as well. Our statement, as it stands today, reads as follows:

We empower activists, through self-awareness and other transformative skills, to be at their highest level of effectiveness through reduced stress, reactivity, and overwhelm, and through enhanced emotional, spiritual and physical well-being. We encourage and support activists to become purposeful agents of change, recognizing that each individual is an indispensable part of our movement.

We urge you to be fearless in the creation of your mission statement. Make sure what you write truly resonates with you on the deepest level and reflects the change you wish to see in the world.

Please share your mission statement with us, either on Facebook (*http://www.facebook.com/BeyondResistance*), Twitter (*@Beyond Resistanc*), or by email (*info@beyondresistancebook.com*).

## Creating a Toolbox

When you are hit with the day's news and find yourself immersed in negativity, clarity about how to respond or act can be elusive. By creating a plan of action, with tools at the ready, you can immediately respond without needing to figure it out in the heat of the moment.

Following the bombing of a Syrian air base after a chemical weapons strike on Syrian civilians by the Assad regime, Donna watched Trump being interviewed by a newswoman who, in her opinion, acted like "a coquettish schoolgirl more concerned with flirting than with asking hard questions." Donna became incensed. "There were a hundred important things she could have asked him and didn't." She thought of all the questions she would have asked if given the chance.

Donna had previously identified tools that she'd feel good about implementing when overwhelm set in, such as acknowledging and naming feelings, writing postcards, and using her breath. Instead of having to figure out how to deal with her emotions in this situation or allowing them to overwhelm her, she was able to go directly to her toolkit and step into action:

First, she acknowledged her feelings of anger, frustration, and incredulity.

She took three deep cleansing breaths to help dissipate the strong emotions.

Next, she used the energy of those emotions productively and wrote a postcard to the interviewer, laying out her concerns and asking why the interviewer hadn't asked the hard questions.

Finally, she took the time to acknowledge herself for doing her "job" of writing postcards, the thing that she had determined was the most effective action she could take at any given moment.

Donna walked away with a clear head, knowing that she may have sent only one postcard, but combined with the postcards of others, it become part of a collective force. She was ready to move on.

## The Bottom Line

Taking action is a powerful way to channel challenging emotions. In this chapter, you have learned how to :

- ▶ Define an overall resistance strategy
- ▶ Identify your targeted area of activism
- ▶ Get in touch with your expansive vision
- ▶ Create a vision board
- ▶ Choose a goal you will commit to that leads toward the fulfilment of your vision
- ▶ Determine the action steps necessary to achieve your goal
- ▶ Create a resistance mission statement

You have experienced the power and honesty of your inner guidance when you become still and ask the right questions. It is always available to serve you and your best interests if you listen to and trust its messages. Connecting to your internal wisdom is a process that doesn't necessarily take hold overnight, so be gentle with yourself as you learn to trust.

In resistance (and life), it is important to stay focused and maintain clear boundaries if you wish to avoid overwhelm. Remember, you now have a template to go back to and use every step of the way. Don't wing it; use it!

CHAPTER 6

# The Fatal Four

### Monkey Chatter

At this point, you may be hearing a little voice whispering, "Who do you think you are? Elizabeth Warren? It's just too hard to change our broken political system," or "You're only one person—you are never going to get enough people out to vote." Sound familiar? Meet your monkey! We all have a monkey that crawls into our heads and torments us from time to time. You know, the one that berates you with "I am not enough"—not good enough, smart enough, rich enough, creative enough, young enough, old enough...the possibilities are endless. If Barack Obama had allowed monkey chatter to dissuade him, he may never have become a US Senator, much less the first African American President of the United States.

If you are taking political action, or even just contemplating it, you may hear the monkey chattering in your ear, telling you all the reasons you can't or shouldn't. You might hear the little rascal say something like, "Be careful. . .if you make your political views known, you may anger people and get into trouble." Your monkey wastes no time running out to warn you. He causes you to doubt yourself, and makes you believe he is protecting you from perceived danger, failure, change, or even success. The reality is that your monkey will only sabotage and limit you, keep you stuck and small, and barrage you with negativity and trepidation. You may dream of running for public office, but that little critter fills your head with the fear of making a fool of yourself or, worse yet, losing. He warns you that it is better to remain in your bubble where it's safe.

In psychology, a metaphor for negative self-talk is that of a human mind filled with hundreds of little monkeys in trees, swinging wildly from thought to thought all day and night, chattering nonstop. While popular belief would offer that the originator of the monkey-mind concept was the Buddha, there is no solid evidence that he coined the term. This image is common to many Eastern religions and has been explored in poetry, drama, and literature for centuries. No matter the source of this concept, these self-defeating thoughts eventually get the better of us.

Monkey loves using shame, foreboding, and terror as tactics, jumping up and down, waving his arms, warning you of all the things you should be wary of—everything that could go wrong. Your monkey may scream at you, impossible to ignore, or take a more subversive approach. Subtler tactics might appear as queasiness in your body or diminished motivation, interest, and joy. Monkey is a master excuse-maker and expert at convincing you of all the reasons you "can't." For example, you may feel excited at the prospect of taking on a leadership position with your local Indivisible chapter, but subsequently, dread sets in. The excitement abates, and you shrink back into your safe place.

What makes monkey's chatter seem so real and ominous? *You believe it!* How can you mitigate his power over you? The first step is awareness—awareness of your monkey, where he comes from, and what he is saying between the lines.

## Monkey and Shadow—A Love Affair

Throughout our lives, we learn from our experiences and develop beliefs about how to avoid pain. Some of what we extrapolate from our experiences is important and useful, but some is not. For example, as a child, maybe you tried and failed at something and were made fun of or shamed for it. You decided that putting yourself out there and risking failure again would be potentially hurtful or devastating. Your monkey grabbed hold of this information and became a hypervigilant hall monitor, jumping up and waving red flags any time you even thought about risking failure again. He said things like: "Hey, what do you think you're doing getting up in front of hundreds of people to make a political speech? Are you nuts? You will look like a fool!" or "You shouldn't make calls on behalf of your candidates because you sound stupid—your calls will just make things worse!"

Monkey loves your shadows. They are his feeding ground, and he thrives on giving voice to them. When you have determined that displaying a specific quality isn't safe, your monkey will sniff out any situation where you might inadvertently exhibit that characteristic and call in the heavy artillery for protection. Your monkey is *always* in pursuit of safety—he never takes a break. He is impeccably trained to look out for potential danger, but there is no nuance in his thinking. He equates risk of any kind with mortal danger. Remember Donna's mean, nasty bitch? Her monkey will try to keep her from being that by all means. Kathy's arrogance? Monkey will stop at nothing to prevent her from being "that."

Donna's friend Lily wanted to give a passionate talk to her local Democratic women's group, but she had never spoken publicly before. Lily had a shadow belief that she was boring and had nothing of substance to offer because she was raised by a father who often dismissed her when she spoke. Lily prepared her talk but was incredibly nervous. Her monkey let her know that she would not do a good job, that people would be bored, that they would think she didn't know what she was talking about. Giving this talk fed into Lily's shadows of being boring and lacking substance; monkey was using it to have a party in her head!

Remember, monkey wants to protect you from that which you most fear. Will you allow him to derail you or will you acknowledge him, remembering that it is merely a distraction and that you are ultimately in control?

## Some ID, Please!

Learning to identify your monkey is an essential step toward emotional freedom. If you can't identify him, he will run the show and wreak havoc without ever being caught. Once you recognize this, you are in a position to stop him. Rather than blindly reacting, you can take a step back, notice the noise, and approach the thoughts from a place of curiosity rather than victimhood, judgment, or even numbness. Recognizing that your monkey is often repetitive and thematic will help you call him out with greater speed and efficiency.

The most effective way to limit the impact of your monkey's incessant negative chatter is to become a conscious observer of your thoughts. You may notice the same derisive narrative repeatedly playing in your head: "You can't do that," "You aren't smart enough," or "Don't even bother. It will never work." You might have a more physical response like a knot in the pit of your stomach or shortness of breath, or you may receive emotional messages of anxiety, sadness, or anger. Laura, an actor, had anxiety pulsing through her brain every day, all day long. She had one anxious thought after another; they controlled her life. Laura spent countless years looking for ways to soothe herself, including alcohol, without success. Through coaching, she learned that the anxiety-producing doomsday voice in her head was her monkey trying to keep her from danger on all fronts.

Laura began to recognize these thoughts for what they were, the product of an overactive monkey trying to keep her safe from the pain of the past, warning: "Don't make a mistake," "Don't be too loud," "Don't take a risk," and "Don't outshine others." When Laura finally shone a spotlight on her monkey and saw him for what he was, an overprotective fraudulent messenger who sabotaged her dreams, she said, "He shrank into the shadows. He is still there, but he no longer holds the same power over me. I am finally free!" With awareness and practice, you can enjoy the same freedom from your monkey.

## Intuition vs. Monkey Chatter

You may wonder how you can distinguish between monkey chatter and intuition. With practice, the difference will become clear. Intuition is an effortless, immediate, and often unreasoned sense of truth. Prince Charles of England once said, "Buried deep within each and every one of us, there is an instinctive, heartfelt awareness that provides—if we allow it to—the most reliable guide as to whether or not our actions are really in the long-term interests of our planet and all the life it supports." We must, he continued, listen "more to the common sense emanating from our hearts." We all have an instinct that is generously willing to offer guidance on both the smallest matters and the grandest plans. If you tend to and respect your intuition, you will have a lifelong resource more valuable than gold. On the other hand, your monkey is an impetuous little scoundrel who keeps you in a state of anxiety, confusion, and overwhelm. He destabilizes and sabotages your best-laid plans and, because he deals in untruths, leaves you in a state of defeat.

The Buddhist perspective recommends quiet meditation as an opportunity to calm anxiety and soften the mind's chatter. According to Robert Wright, a journalist with *Vox*, the day after Trump was elected, the meditation app Headspace had a burst in traffic. It was a very specific burst—a growth of 44 percent in the use of a feature called SOS, which is designed to calm people during times of great stress. He states: "Meditation—mindfulness meditation, in particular—can be a weapon against Trump, a tool for active resistance against the forces he represents." Approaching the day with calm and mindfulness allows you to stay open to new ideas or resolutions to challenges. Monkey chatter doesn't completely disappear, but you gain the ability to choose whether to believe and act upon it or not.

## Monkey Chatter Journaling Exercise

- Spend three days simply observing what your monkey has to say about your activism or self-care plans. Do you find he repeats himself? Does his message sound familiar? Write down when he shows up and what he has to say.
- Connect within and explore the emotions, feelings, or thoughts that appear when your monkey causes self-doubt.
- Think of a time when you allowed your monkey to get the better of you, a time when he sabotaged your plans, ideas, or dreams. What were his tactics and words of warning? How did it feel to succumb to his pressure: demoralizing, disempowering, discouraging?
- Think of another time when your monkey *tried* to push you off track, but you resisted his tactics and moved forward anyway. How did that feel: empowering, exciting, courageous?
- Journal briefly about what it might be like to be released from the tyranny of your monkey's chatter. What would be different if you were able to acknowledge the chatter but not react to it or be the victim of it? Would you accomplish more of your goals? Would you be more at peace or have greater self-esteem?
- What would allow you to have the faith and courage to move beyond the warnings that your monkey throws at you? Recognizing that your thoughts are just thoughts—not necessarily truth? Learning more about shadows and monkey chatter through coaching?

Giving your monkey some love and understanding to help him calm down?

## Summing Up Monkey Chatter

After a while, with practice, you will be able to remember quickly that your monkey, while trying to keep you safe, is not in possession of all the facts. He bases his warnings and "advice" on old stories and protective mechanisms that are not in your best interests. Therefore, treat your monkey with kindness and understanding, thank him for trying to protect you, but let him know, "I've got this." Eventually, you will be able to silence him almost before he opens his mouth.

## Comparison and Judgment

*Comparison is the death of joy.*
—Unknown

Your monkey loves that you compare yourself to others. He delights in your judgment of yourself and everyone else. It's another tactic he employs to get you to stop dead in your tracks when he is frightened. He is an opportunist who will jump right in to shine a spotlight on any shadow belief you hold; he is a hook to keep you in check. A shadow belief of "I'm not good enough" becomes the root of the little voice telling you, "He is doing so much more than I," or "I'll never make a big difference." All judgments are self-defeating and most often not based in fact. Here's the thing: even though your judgment meter may, on occasion, come up in your favor, it's still a no-win situation. The temporary "win" may give you a momentary boost, but the feeling cannot sustain itself because it is not based on truth. The story you tell yourself is just that—a story, a belief about the situation.

The person you perceive as doing so much better than you may, in fact, be comparing herself to others and believe she is coming up short, or she may be working herself to the bone, certain she needs to prove something to the world, while you are content and balanced. The person whom you judge yourself to be better than may be satisfied and exactly where he or she wants to be. The point is, you don't know someone else's reality, and the comparison you make is likely filtered through your shadow beliefs and imaginings about another's situation.

If you are someone who harshly judges yourself, you may be aware that you do the same to others. Self-judgment usually begins with judging others. And when you judge others, concern invariably creeps in that others are judging you in return. To defend against this, you preemptively judge yourself as a defense mechanism. Henrik Edberg, creator of *The Positivity Blog*, writes, "In my experience, the way you behave and think toward others seems to have a big, big effect on how you behave toward yourself and think about yourself. Judge and criticize people more and you tend to judge and criticize yourself more (often almost automatically). Be kinder to other people and help them and you tend to be kinder and more helpful to yourself."

When you judge yourself or others, you are not in personal integrity. Remember, integrity is about presence, listening to your inner wisdom and acting and behaving in alignment with your truth. No one's truth is that they need to be meaner or compare themselves to others. No one's inner wisdom tells them to tear themselves and others down. So why do we do it? You are either looking to create safety by judging yourself first, before anyone else has the opportunity, or by validating yourself as okay or "better than."

We all experience moments of insecurity when it comes to our accomplishments or lack thereof. But this is a learned behavior—we were not born criticizing or judging ourselves—and, as such, we can unlearn it. Start to observe where you are judging or negating yourself or others throughout the day. When you notice yourself in judgment, gently (without judging!) choose to release it and affirm to yourself that you no longer need judgment as a defense mechanism. What you and others have to give is enough. Judgment does not serve you. You will be happier, lighter, and more empowered when you let go of the need to compare and judge.

Sharon, a high-level fashion executive, grew up in New York City, which she describes as the capital of judgment and comparison. "I grew up comparing myself to everyone else. My self-worth depended on how I measured up, and how I felt about myself was dependent on how the scales tipped in any given situation. If I felt prettier than someone else, I felt great! If I felt unattractive compared to another person, I felt diminished and unworthy. The same held true for my self-comparison on any number of other fronts: clothing, apartment, vacations, and even family. This was a miserable way to live—constantly judging myself against others—rolling the dice to see if I came out on top." As time went on, Sharon's judgments evolved. She was now comparing herself in other ways as well. Was her job better or worse than someone else's? Sharon had a dream of running for public office. But every time she touched upon the issue in her mind, the comparisons began. She was certain that others running for office had more to offer than she could. She put them on a pedestal, and her self-judgment led her to believe she could never win. Convinced of her inadequacies, Sharon allowed years to pass while her dream remained unfulfilled.

Frustrated, Sharon began a coaching relationship with Donna. She learned that her comparisons and judgments were keeping her boxed in and small. Her plans and dreams rarely materialized because self-judgment stopped her every time. Sharon began to observe the many ways she sabotaged herself with her never-ending judgment.

The first step to changing any pattern is awareness, which Sharon now possessed. The second step is choice. Sharon made the conscious choice to recognize when she was in a place of judgment and remind herself that it was a self-sabotaging, false, and destructive path. She reaffirmed her core belief in herself and her conviction that each person has something of value to offer. Finally, Sharon practiced and broke her habit of defaulting to judgment. It took some time, but after a while, she noticed that most judgment had stopped, and when it did appear, she recognized it and rewrote the script. Coaching enabled Sharon to quiet her judgments, monkey chatter, and shadow beliefs. The result? She is running for her local school board! She thinks about running for higher office and, having let go of her comparisons and judgments, knows this is no longer simply a dream.

## Comparison and Judgment Journaling Exercise

• Observe your comparison and judgment patterns, thoughts, and behaviors for several days and answer the following questions:

• How do you feel when you compare yourself to others? Whether it's another resister or activist, a stranger, an acquaintance, a celebrity, a good friend, or even a politician, what feelings are generated within you? Inferiority? Superiority? How often do you judge or criticize people?

• How do your comparisons and judgments keep you stuck and prevent you from moving forward in life? How do they cripple your ability to achieve what you say you want?

• Do your comparisons sometimes motivate you? Observe how this is a temporary fix and journal about how to create motivation from within rather than needing to find it outside of yourself.

• What would be possible if you chose to release comparison and judgment from your life?

## Summing up Comparison and Judgment

Negating ourselves and our accomplishments, or falsely boosting our egos with comparisons, serves no positive purpose and holds us back from becoming all that we can be. Comparing yourself to another is a fantasy. At best, you may gain a temporary false sense of security, but you are also guaranteed to lose joy, self-esteem, and connectedness. Is it worth it?

## Excuses

*Excuses are lies we tell ourselves so that it doesn't have to be our fault.*
-Chris Creed, blogger and photographer

We all do it—make excuses because we believe they will protect or safeguard us from the reactions of others. Did you ever have dinner planned with a friend and cancel at the last minute, offering up a headache as your excuse instead of owning up to just not being in the mood?

Excuses keep us from being held responsible. They declare to the world, "It wasn't my fault!" Trump is an expert at this: "It's just locker room talk," "There's blame on both sides." Excuses are rationalizations we make to justify behavior. We've all been late and blamed traffic because we didn't want our boss or friend to be angry with us. Excuses also provide cover. For example, Trump used an IRS audit as an excuse not to release his taxes. Finally, excuses are a means of placing blame on something other than ourselves. Trump's blaming the Democrats for his legislative failures is a perfect example.

The reasons we create excuses are many and varied, but they are always based on fear of potential outcomes. These may include failure, success, embarrassment or humiliation, change, uncertainty, responsibility, or punishment.

Fear often results from of a lack of information, understanding or clarity, resources, experience, or objectivity. It is a vicious cycle:

if you lack these things, your confidence wanes and your monkey takes charge, most likely dissuading you from acting to achieve your goal. Consequently, you make excuses about why it wasn't your fault to make yourself feel better and boost your battered self-esteem. The irony is, while it appears you are taking care of or protecting yourself when you make an excuse, your sense of security is a false one. You disempower yourself each time you do not take ownership of your part in any given situation. The damage of this disempowerment is long-lasting, while the benefit achieved from the excuse is usually temporary.

What are your "go to" excuses? Do you use them to explain and complain about how and why circumstances are as they are or why something is not your fault? Time and money are the most common excuses. But they can also sound like, "I'm not motivated today," or "I'm only one person—what difference can I make?" Sometimes, excuses are justified: "My child needs to go to the doctor," or "I have to travel an hour to and from my job every day." However, even if these declarations are true, they are still excuses if you use them to avoid responsibility. If you decide based on conscious choice and in integrity with your truth, it is not an excuse.

Making the decision to let go of your excuses is a radical step toward self-empowerment. Each time you avoid responsibility, you give your power away and declare you are a helpless victim. Once you are trapped in a cycle of excuse-making, it's difficult to find your way out. When you acknowledge your part in any given situation, you affirm that you are in control of your choices.

## Excuses Journaling Exercise

Observe your excuse pattern for a few days and answer the following questions:

• What are some of your favorite excuses? When it comes time to participate in a march, what do you tell yourself? ("Someone else will do it." "I'm too busy today." "One person won't make a difference.")

• Why are you making these excuses? How or from what or whom do you believe they will protect you?

• What are the consequences of your excuses? How do they keep you stuck and prevent you from moving forward? How do they cripple your ability to achieve what you say you want?

• How are your excuses causing you to settle for less than you can be?

• How would letting go of excuse-making benefit you today, next week, next month, and in the years ahead?

• Are you willing to make the commitment to let go of your excuses and stand in personal integrity and responsibility?

## Summing up Excuses

Success in any endeavor requires a commitment to change and often a period of discomfort as you venture into unfamiliar territory. The consequences of continued excuse-making are many, from a persistent negative outlook and extensive regrets to an absence of personal growth and an unfulfilling life. To overcome your excuses, you must admit that you are making them in the first place. This is not always an easy task when the practice of excuse-making is deeply ingrained. Pay attention to your excuses; they will help you identify potential blind spots. For example, you may want to make calls to your elected representative, but adopt the excuse that you don't have the time. If you look more closely, you might find that this is a cover-up for a lack of confidence in your ability to sound intelligent about the issue you want to discuss in the call. Your excuse is a clue that there is something more to be explored. When you find and address the root cause of an excuse, you make the shift from victim to champion.

## Self-Righteousness

Self-righteousness makes our Fatal Four list because of the damage it causes in our lives. Self-righteousness keeps us stuck in our point of view, unwilling to even consider other viewpoints. In the spirit of total transparency, we must admit that this is a tough subject for us now. We are both keenly aware of the pitfalls of self-righteousness but have yet to master our own personal indignation over practically everything Trump-related (the man, his social media habits, policies, supporters, etc.) because, let's face it . . . *we're right and they're wrong!* We are wagering a guess that you are in a similar place, so we will share with you what we know about self-righteousness and hope it will, at the very least, provide you a new perspective.

Self-righteousness is described as an attitude or display of moral superiority derived from a sense that one's beliefs, actions, or affiliations are of greater value than those of others. Holier-than-thou thoughts, such as: "They don't know what they are talking about,"

## The Fatal Four

"He's doing it wrong," "She deserved it," or, "That's so inappropriate," are usually clues that you are in a self-righteous mind-set. It is more than simply having an opinion. Self-righteous people are intolerant of the opinions and behaviors of others. They are in a constant power struggle. By pointing out the errors of others, or even making up "alternative facts," they attempt to position themselves as "better than."

Our own self-righteousness tells us that Kellyanne Conway offers perhaps the quintessential example of self-righteous behavior. In our view, she oozes self righteousness every time she opens her mouth. She is not even afraid to throw in a few "untruths" to support her righteous positions—remember, she was the creator of the now-infamous term "alternative facts." During a *Meet the Press* interview, Kellyanne offered up her self-righteousness while defending former White House press secretary Sean Spicer's false claims of large attendance at Trump's inauguration and stated that Spicer was providing "alternative facts." Chuck Todd, her interviewer, responded incredulously, "Look, alternative facts are not facts. They're falsehoods." However, she would not be deterred. Perhaps it is Kellyanne's self-righteousness that spurs the maelstrom of negative responses and impassioned reactions she receives in general. And, as is evident from this example of our self-righteousness about her self-righteousness, there is self-righteous indignation flying all over the place!

Does having principles and integrity preclude you from listening or being open to another's point of view? Self-righteousness should be in no way confused with taking a moral stand or acting from a place of personal integrity. It has little to do with either party's being right or wrong. Both are right from their perspective. Pro-lifers are in integrity with their beliefs and take a moral stand when they protest abortion—this in and of itself is not self-righteous behavior. It becomes self-righteous when fingers are pointed, morals are declared superior, and there is no willingness to acknowledge or discuss any other point of view.

Many of us have thrown away relationships (or unfriended Facebook connections) because we are unwilling to move even slightly off our high horse to hear what another has to say. What might moving off our high horse look like? Sarah Silverman, comedian, actor, and no stranger to taboo subjects, is a great example. She has created a new Hulu TV show called *I Love You, America,* where she lets go of her self-righteousness and seeks to find common ground with Trump supporters. Silverman states, "I've never been so aware of the truth of the concept of 'liberal bubble.' I'm taking it to heart, and I want to get outside of it." What might be possible if we all gave ourselves a chance to open to this kind of interaction? What stops us?

We hold on to self-righteousness because we humans love to be right. We are frightened that if we open ourselves up to another way of looking at things, we risk our world crashing down, thrusting us into a tailspin of uncertainty. Thus, we cling to what we believe with white knuckles.

Trump has demonstrated his need to be right and prove others wrong time and time again. His need to convince us that his inauguration attendance was bigger than President Obama's led him to post a photograph in the West Wing where those skeptical of his "unbelievable, perhaps record-setting" turnout would see it every day. After the Trump- endorsed, alleged pedophile Roy Moore's defeat in Alabama's special election, Trump tweeted: "The reason I originally endorsed Luther Strange (and his numbers went up mightily), is that I said Roy Moore will not be able to win the General Election. I was right!"

The cost of Trump's self-righteousness to the American people is mammoth, not least of which is heightened conflict, ever-widening polarization, and contempt between left and right. This polarization has led to the breakdown of relationships, empathy, communication, and even effective government.

We have both found ourselves angry and frustrated after a conversation turns into a confrontation with a Trump supporter, hurling "facts" at each other, neither listening nor connecting with one another. We have lost a lot of time and peace of mind digging our heels in and becoming upset. But it's our well-being and effectiveness as resisters that take the biggest hit during these encounters. We now ask ourselves, "If all I get out of this is the satisfaction of saying I'm right, but it costs me _____, is it worth it?" We must each answer that question for ourselves.

## Self-Righteousness Journaling Exercise

For several days, observe your words, thoughts, and emotions during your interactions with others and answer the following questions:

- What beliefs do you hold onto with self-righteousness? What do you believe is the absolute truth about Trump?

- How does self-righteousness show up in your mind and body? Are you triggered or tense? Do you experience shortness of breath or rapid heartbeat?
- How do you feel when you are indignant about something or someone?
- What are your motives for holding on to your self-righteous positions? How or from what or whom do you believe they will protect you?
- What are the costs of holding onto these righteous positions?
- How does your self-righteousness prevent you from moving forward?
- How would letting go of your self-righteousness benefit you today, next week, next month, and in the years to come?

## Summing Up Self-Righteousness

Self-righteousness is a sure way to separate ourselves from others. It leaves little room for understanding or compromise and invites contempt into our lives. How do you feel when you are on the receiving end of someone's self-righteous behavior? Are you inspired to listen with an open mind? Do you like the person or want to hear what they have to say? Any time we attempt to convince another of the righteousness of our position but have not heard, recognized, understood, or valued them as individuals, they will, most assuredly, not hear us either. There is always a choice as to how you present your views: a little humility and honest exploration of your true motivation and another's point of view can go a long way in finding some common ground. The ultimate question is whether our self-righteousness will move us forward as a nation or keep us stuck in our indignation and separateness. What do you think?

## The Bottom Line

This chapter has shed light on four aspects of transformation that have changed countless lives. A deeper understanding of the subconscious ways you self-sabotage, and an awareness of the monkey chatter, comparison and judgment, excuses, and self-righteousness that keep you from accomplishing all you desire will provide you the ability to get back in the driver's seat of your life. With consciousness, vigilance, commitment, and practice, you will quickly notice substantial changes and a greater sense of freedom.

CHAPTER 7

# From Finger-Pointing to Freedom

*Not forgiving is like drinking rat poison
and then waiting for the rat to die.*
—Anne Lamott, author

Although you may not realize it, grudge-holding is an insidious form of self-sabotage. Forgiveness and letting go of anger, possibly held on to years after the fact, are tremendous steps toward emotional freedom and personal empowerment. They are acts of self-care. Hurt and anger directed at another or ourselves are psychic blocks. They keep us chained to the event that caused our pain, and they waste precious emotional energy and time. Right about now, you may be thinking, "No way! I will never forgive _____ for _____. It was awful and they do not deserve forgiveness!" But hang in there for a moment and let us explain.

Think of forgiveness as something you do for you. It is not about the person who wronged you, nor is it condoning what they did. It's about unlocking the chains that keep you shackled to both the past and the pain. You may be adamant that the wound you have experienced should not be released without punishment of the transgressor, but, we promise, the only way to find freedom is through forgiveness. You may believe you must cling to your anger and resentment to punish the person who hurt you. But, as Anne Lamott reminds us, the only person you are hurting is you! Take a moment to connect with the resentment you hold for someone who has hurt you. How does it feel in your body—suffocating, constricting, upsetting, anger-producing? By consistently returning to it, you stay stuck in those feelings and re-injure yourself over and over again. In his *Psychology Today* article, "Chains of Resentment," Steven Stosny, PhD, founder of CompassionPower, shares how a member of a class he taught described the effects of resentment. "Dragging the chain of resentment through life is like carrying around a bag of horse manure." Okay, he did not say "manure." Stosny continues: "You want to smear the bag of horse do-do in the face of the person you resent. So, you carry it around, waiting for the opportunity, and carry it around, and carry it around, and carry it around. And who stinks?"

According to Clifford B. Edwards, author of *The Forgiveness Handbook*, "Forgiveness liberates you from the oppressive burdens of negative judgments, unresolved emotions, and the chafing restrictions of limiting beliefs from the past. You forgive so that you can be clean mentally and emotionally"—and we would add spiritually to this—"so that you can move forward in your life powerfully, with purpose, clarity and confidence. You forgive so that you can be free, fully self-expressed, and able to achieve your dreams."

*From Finger-Pointing to Freedom*

But why, even when we say we want to move on and let go, do we remain stuck? The answer is that we have been trained throughout our lives to hold grudges. It's a constant theme in our music, soap operas, and films. All children witness their parents, teachers, and friends react to being "wronged" and unwittingly take on their habits. Subconsciously, many of us believe there is some benefit to adopting the label of being the person betrayed by a loved one, cheated out of a promotion, treated unfairly by a coworker, etc. We want everyone to know about it, so we gather evidence and enroll others into our sorrowful story. By showing the world that we were so obviously victimized, we announce to all that we deserve understanding, kindness, or special treatment. This is what we "get" out of the situation. As Alanis Morissette sings in her wonderful song "This Grudge" on her album *So-Called Chaos*, "This [grudge]—has served me greatly, ever the victim."(We recommend listening to this song to hear more about how grudge-holding holds us back.)

And you carry around a sack of manure on your back, sometimes for years or even a lifetime. You adopt it as a part of your identity and may even wear it as a badge of honor, proving to the world that you have suffered greatly. The irony is that displaying the evidence of your suffering does not accomplish the goal of making you feel less hurt; the burden you carry only weighs you down. And it grows heavier over time.

Look closely and you will see that grudge-holding keeps you out of integrity. Integrity comes from your heart. Grudges are your monkey at work, filling you with stories of how you have been wronged, continuing the cycle of pain. When you hold a grievance, kindness, understanding, and empathy for others—and yourself—are far away.

## I Hate You

Many of us are experiencing enormous rage toward Trump, his administration, and its supporters. Every day it seems we are provided another reason to hate—pulling out of the Paris Accord; attempting to ban transgender people from the military; dismantling DACA; pardoning Joe Arpaio, the ex-sheriff who illegally rounded up undocumented workers through racial profiling; placing white supremacists and those protesting them on equal moral footing; trying to destroy Obamacare; passing tax reform that heavily favors the wealthy, and the list goes on.

It is important to understand the difference between disagreement, resentment, and contempt. The first allows a window for dialogue or an exchange of ideas. Resentment and contempt do not. We may be filled with rage and contempt for Trump supporters and what we believe they are doing to our country, but all we have written about forgiveness still holds true. Think about it from the perspective of your own internal well-being. Does grudge-holding serve you? If we wish to bridge the political chasm, will we not need to learn to forgive and talk with one another?

We have focused a great deal on forgiving others, but we need to stress the importance of self-forgiveness as well. It may be hard to forgive someone else, but it may be even harder to forgive yourself for any number of perceived wrongs—for allowing hate and resentment into your life; for blocking your peace of mind with continuous ruminations over choices you've made; for wasting time with anger. There are many things for which you can forgive yourself. With quiet reflection, gentleness, and inquiry, you will come to understand where self-forgiveness may be warranted. Think of forgiveness as an ongoing process, not a one-time event.

Donna feels the election has changed her. Hate, a word she seldom used, has been in heavy rotation since November 9, 2016. Swearing was not a part of her everyday life, but she now says she "swears like a sailor." It's not who she wants to be nor does it create the world she wants to live in, particularly when she believes that her words form the reality she inhabits. Donna concedes that she dehumanizes those she considers "deplorable." Clearly, this will not forward her deepest commitment to living in a world of peace and harmony. This hate has been a source of shame, and Donna recognizes the need for a good dose of self-forgiveness—for her feelings of contempt, and for using language that drags her and those around her down. She began the process of self-forgiveness by affirming her desire to forgive herself and journaling about the situation. Now she consciously reframes her words and has committed to using more peaceful and supportive language.

## Forgiveness Journaling Exercise

Write out the story you have created around a situation about which you have been holding a grudge. What happened? How were you wronged?

- Ask yourself what you have gained from holding on to the story you created. Sympathy, attention, or compassion from others? Do you get to be right and make the other person wrong?

- Release the need for these perceived benefits and focus on giving yourself the attention, love, and understanding you desire. How might you begin this process—with meditation, affirmations, journaling, or some spiritual self-care?
- Acknowledge that you have no control over another's actions but can choose to give yourself the gift of being responsible for your reactions.
- Ask yourself what action you can take to initiate the process of letting go. Begin to release your story and the feelings associated with it to affirm that it no longer serves you.

## The Bottom Line

Holding a grudge eats away at us. It keeps us in a state of emotional turmoil and lessens our power as activists. To be effective, we do not have to make Trump and his supporters our enemies; this mindset only weighs us down (remember the sack of poo?). We promise that if you choose to take up forgiveness as a tool, you'll experience a great deal more joy. As a final word, we offer this prayer written by Rabbi David Ingber, founder of Romemu, an egalitarian Jewish community for body, heart, and spirit:

May the Source of Love awaken in me the capacity to forgive those who supported a candidate who has plunged us into darkness. May the Source of Love awaken in me the capacity to see them as human, to extend myself to understand their perspective, and to share with them a different perspective. And may the Source of Love awaken in them a recognition that our country deserves much better, so that we may all learn the skillful means that lead to greater understanding and, eventually, to real forgiveness. Amen.

CHAPTER 8

# Can We Tawk?

*Change happens by listening and then starting a dialogue with the people who are doing something you don't believe is right.*
—Jane Goodall, primatologist

Most people would agree that we are a deeply divided nation. Trump seized upon and exploited this division all the way to the White House. Even during the Bush years, Republicans and Democrats were at least able to dialogue, dine together, and compromise. These kinds of exchanges no longer occur. Lines have been drawn, fingers are pointed like guns, and there is blame and disdain all around.

Those of us on the left are frustrated and angry because we *know* we are on the right side of history. We *know* without a doubt that we are standing up for the little guy, for the rights of women, for education, for the environment, for immigrants, for people of color, for all. We don't even want to engage with *them* because they don't listen. In other words, they don't accept our version of reality. We project all sorts of nasty characteristics on them and are enraged that they believe verifiable lies. But we must remember that Trump supporters believe in their "rightness," too. Osama bin Laden was also sure he was right.

We have insulated and isolated ourselves through our social circles and social and news media. Do you find yourself "preaching to the choir" much of the time? If we only keep talking to ourselves, how will we get anywhere? It's a conundrum that will take some big people dropping their self-righteousness and coming together. Is it possible? Of course it is. Are we willing to do what it takes? Each of us must answer that for ourselves. One thing is certain: If you try to convince someone with facts or other information about the righteousness of your position but you demonstrate little interest in their viewpoint, it is unlikely they will listen to you.

It will take heroic efforts, or perhaps a cataclysmic event, to bring us back together. We must each commit to finding the common thread that inextricably binds us together as Americans. Could our commonality be that we are all human beings with a need to survive on this planet; that we all want to be safe, loved, and healthy? Does it take recognizing that without each other, we won't make it? How are we to know this if we do not talk with one another?

Texas Congressmen Beto O'Rourke, Democrat, and Will Hurd, Republican, are great examples of what might be possible if we open our minds, hearts, and ears. In March of 2017, because of inclement weather and canceled flights, O'Rourke and Hurd drove from Texas to Washington, DC, together to get back in time to cast their votes for pending legislation. They decided to livestream their 1,600 miles of banter and heavy policy discussion. They discovered they share some things in common: they both prefer *Star Wars* to *Star Trek*,

*Can We Tawk?*

they have similar tastes in music, and they both like Mexican food. Getting to know each other in this way formed the basis of a new friendship from which they were able to talk about more difficult topics such as veterans' services, Medicaid, immigration, and frustrations with the partisan fighting in Washington.

Sometimes we avoid dialogue because we are in a place of fear and self-righteousness, unwilling to consider another's thoughts or feelings, or because we can't deal with the anxiety it produces. But perhaps we are cheating ourselves out of a profound or life-altering experience by hiding ourselves from "the boogeyman." Recently, businessman and former US Congressional candidate Paul Chabot formed a new real estate company called Conservative Move. Its mission is to help right-leaning families and businesses relocate from blue states to the Lone Star state—so that they no longer need to "suffer" being around "liberal snowflakes." The company motto is "Helping families move Right." That is certainly one way to avoid dialogue with people who hold different points of view from your own! But separating ourselves this way will only widen and deepen the chasm that already exists, making it eventually impossible to heal the rift.

How can we be open to others' perspectives and listen to what they are saying without becoming unhinged? We can leave frustration, finger-pointing, contempt, and anger aside and connect from a place of curiosity, openness, compassion, understanding, and love. Recently on an episode of the TV series *Big Little Lies*, one of the lead characters, Renata, was sure that her daughter was being bullied by a little boy in her class whose mother was Jane. Jane was positive her son did not bully Renata's daughter. Renata's rhetoric and behavior toward Jane were vicious; her fear and self-righteousness were palpable. Finally, Jane ventured to Renata's home, knowing she would not be welcomed. Courageously, Jane explained that she understood that Renata must be feeling the same way that she was feeling—scared. Now, this was TV, but after that, they were fast friends. What would be possible if we could walk a mile in someone else's shoes?

We encourage our clients to approach stressful situations or confrontations by asking themselves, "What is my goal? What is the result to which I am committed in this conversation or circumstance?" It's imperative that you are honest and gentle with yourself when answering this question. When you are confronted with someone who has another point of view, is your goal to get the upper hand or be right? Is it to be liked or avoid conflict? If you engaged from a place of personal integrity, what would your goal be? What would it look like, or feel like, if you began and ended every conversation from a place of compassion and openness?

## Listening

*When you talk, you are only repeating what you already know.*
*But if you listen, you may learn something.*
—J.P. McEvoy, author

Have you ever been in a political conversation with someone who holds a different viewpoint and found you were both more invested in being right than listening to each other? Have you shared a thought, idea, or opinion and been cut off by someone who jumped in with his or her own? Being interrupted is something that most women are particularly familiar with. It was reported on *Vox* that Trump interrupted Hillary Clinton fifty-one times during one of the presidential debates and, counting the moderator, she was interrupted a total of seventy times!

Being heard and acknowledged is a fundamental need of humans, yet we so often do not hear or acknowledge one another. Most of us were not taught the importance of listening or even how to listen, but listening is an essential part of any discussion. It establishes an environment of safety and leads to more trust in the relationship and the exchange. Without a level of compassion and open-mindedness, we have very little chance of having meaningful dialogue.

How we listen can be affected by a variety of factors. Sometimes it's easier to attack than to sit down and have a genuine exchange of ideas. Shadows—possibly a need to show that you are smart or funny—can cause you to care more about whether your response is brilliant or humorous than about what the other person is saying. Self-righteousness may cause you to reject outright a point of view that differs from your own—it's so easy to get on our high horses about Trump. Emotions can overwhelm our ability to listen. If something you hear feels threatening—someone advocating fracking, for example—your anger may take over, and it's nearly impossible to listen effectively when you are angry. Learning to navigate all these potential roadblocks to listening takes practice and persistence.

When speaking with someone, do you really listen or are you more focused on your response? Are you fully present or are you drifting off, thinking about what you will have for dinner? Are you silently judging them and what they are saying? If so, is this how you want to be treated when you are speaking?

Presence is the key to listening. You do a disservice to yourself and others when you withhold your full attention. You miss opportunities to connect honestly and fully. And if you aren't listening with openness and curiosity, chances are your partner will respond in kind. If you give the gift of your full attention, even when you disagree, it is very likely you will receive the same. And, isn't being heard what we all want?

Listening doesn't require relinquishing your viewpoint. It may feel threatening because of a subconscious fear that you will never get your point across, or worse, that you may begin to question yourself or even lose confidence in your opinion. There is nothing wrong with questioning—it can be an opportunity for growth. Can you trust that your opportunity to speak will arise at the perfect time? What if listening is the only way for us to begin to heal the rift in this country?

## Dialogue Journaling Exercise

**Part 1.** Observe yourself in conversation with others for one day and journal about the following:

Do I make eye contact with whomever I am speaking to?

Do I interrupt?

Are thoughts racing in my mind as another is speaking? Am I thinking about my response or my next vacation?

Am I trying to "fix" things?

Do I invite others to share their opinions?

**Part 2.** In your communications with others, focus for one day on listening attentively. If your attention drifts or you find yourself jumping ahead to your response, come back to what the other person is saying. Journal about the following:

What observations did I have?

How did it feel to listen deeply?

Were there any surprises?

Did my new awareness impact the way other people communicated with me?

By listening to others more deeply, did I learn anything new?

## Confirmation Bias

Confirmation bias is the tendency to look for and interpret evidence as confirmation of one's existing beliefs or theories. Kathy holds the belief that Republicans are selfish and mean-spirited and Democrats are compassionate and caring. When she encounters a Republican who is not empathetic, she sees that as validation of her existing belief. However, when she meets Republicans who express compassionate views, she generally dismisses them as anomalies and thinks privately that they are not "real" Republicans. On the other hand, when Kathy meets Democrats who are neither kind nor compassionate, she makes an excuse for them—maybe they are having a bad day—or ignores this information altogether because it does not support her already-held beliefs.

There is a deep split in this country on the issue of gun control.

We are divided into those who believe that guns protect them and prevent violence and those who believe guns endanger them by encouraging violence. Both sides set out to corroborate their beliefs. Gun owners watching Fox News or reading Breitbart News Network on the web will see and hear stories that give them all the proof they need to support their point of view. Those of us opposed to gun violence will subconsciously seek out support for our view that guns are killing people faster than cancer or heart attacks.

Why is it important to understand confirmation bias? Because we all face it. We can each find ourselves in a bubble if we do not take steps to be vigilant and aware of both the beliefs we hold and the ways we subconsciously strive to validate them. There is a great cost to confirmation bias for the American people and our democracy because it prevents us from looking at issues objectively. With the blinders of confirmation bias, we miss valuable information and opportunities that could assist us in making better choices.

## Contempt

We've shared with you how contempt shows up in self-righteousness and prevents us from finding forgiveness for others, but it can also be a deal-breaker in communication. Arthur Brooks, the author of eleven books and president of the conservative think tank American Enterprise Institute (AEI), said, "The real problem in American politics today is not anger, it's contempt. Contempt is the conviction of the worthlessness of another human being. Unlike anger, which can be resolved, contempt leads to permanent estrangement." Brooks consulted his friend, the Dalai Lama, to understand what he could do when he felt disdain and contempt for another. The answer? "Show warm-heartedness toward those for whom you feel contempt." Perhaps you are thinking to yourself, "Easy for the Dalai Lama to say!" We understand.

How do you talk to someone (a Trump supporter?) you can't stand, and think is crazy and effed up? Honestly, this is a question that we have both pondered and racked our brains over for some time. In fact, writing this section of the book has been one of our greatest challenges. The truth is, we don't have a definitive answer, only some thoughts about how we might all reach the other side.

Contempt has become a normal part of our political discourse, and at this point, there is more than enough to go around on all sides. It's being used as a weapon. The trouble, though, is that contempt cannot be fought with more contempt; meeting contempt with contempt only legitimizes its presence in the public arena. We believe a better strategy is to reject contempt on its face. Becoming aware of its destructiveness and being vigilant in recognizing contempt when it arises are a start. We must affirm our rejection of it even when we may not have another or better response with which to replace it. This is a practice, one that will certainly not provide an immediate outcome, but we believe that with awareness and choice we can turn the tide on contempt over time and repair the fabric that holds us together as a nation.

## Tools and Strategies for Dialoguing

Van Jones, political commentator, host of *The Messy Truth* and founder of #LoveArmy, writes, "Our challenge to you is to talk to a friend or family member who has different political views than you have. Be curious. Ask questions about anything that doesn't sound right to you. But don't just fight back. Try to listen. Be passionate, but be compassionate, too." He offers the following guidelines:

Listen with empathy: Give your full, undivided attention and listen deeply. Try to understand where they're coming from. Look the person in the eye, listen with your whole body. Don't just think about the next thing you want to say or how to win the debate. Don't be judgmental—even if you strongly disagree, hear them out. See this as an opportunity to do some research and learn something new. You're trying to understand. Try repeating back what they said and see if you got it right. Give them a chance to clarify.

Speak authentically and honestly about your feelings: Share your views but don't regurgitate talking points. What are your hopes? What are your fears? Why is it important to you to talk to them about this?

Expect to be surprised: Be curious. Don't assume you already know what they're going to say. Don't presume you understand them. Give them the opportunity to surprise you.

Make a plan: Ask a friend to support you. Make a plan with them about who you might talk to, where you'll meet, how you'll start and end the conversation. Maybe even practice. Get together again after you have your conversation to debrief about what happened.

Be comfortable with silence: Silence is ok. It will give you a chance to gather your thoughts, reflect, and be intentional about how the conversation continues.

Breathe: If you feel yourself getting upset or frustrated, don't forget to breathe.

Know your limits: Don't push yourself too far. Know when you're triggered. Take a deep breath or go to the bathroom. If you aren't able to get centered again, have a plan to wrap up the conversation. If you're able, continue it another time. Don't push yourself so far that the conversation ends up creating more division.

## The Bottom Line

Perhaps communication is and always has been the greatest challenge in our nation's history. It is our desire that what you have learned in this chapter helps you to shift from a triggered reaction to a considered response in all your communications, particularly with those with whom you have differing political opinions. There are many tools available online to further support you in dialogue and active listening skills, and we encourage you to seek them out. Having greater understanding of concepts such as shadow, projection, monkey chatter, confirmation bias, and forgiveness will support you in seeing our common humanity and experiencing less reactive communication with others.

# Epilogue

Dear Reader,

Writing this book has renewed our faith in the power of the tools and principles we coach and live by and their relevance in any given situation. While you may have originally picked up this book to help you cope with your feelings about Trump, you will put it down with a toolbox full of tools to use in your resistance and throughout your life. Living in integrity, listening deeply, and trusting and acting upon your inner wisdom are skills that will provide you with the priceless gift of empowered, authentic living. Creating and following through on a plan that aligns with your vision will lead you to the fulfillment of dreams you may previously not have thought possible. Having a greater awareness and understanding of your subconscious—your shadows, projections, self-righteousness, grudge-holding, and monkey chatter—will allow you to step beyond perceived limitations. As you practice your newly found knowledge and skills, you will discover that you are less reactive to Trump and his supporters, and that you are no longer at the mercy of the world around you. And finally, understanding the importance of self-care will help you to remain in integrity, create boundaries, and take care of yourself on a whole new level.

We've written a great deal about our devastation over the election of Trump. Do we believe there is positive change as a result of this election? Of course. We have witnessed and been a part of an awakening that is awe-inspiring. We, members of the resistance and the Democratic party, are no longer complacent about the status quo; we are called to participate where many of us had been previously sitting on the sidelines. We are seeing the results of this involvement in local elections across the country, such as in Alabama and Virginia. We've been awakened to the depths of the racism that has festered beneath the veil of tolerance and political correctness and stood up to it. We are now open to the idea that certain of our long-held views and values may have pushed us to this critical point and that there must be consideration of a broader perspective than our own if we wish to thrive as a nation. We understand that we must be the change we wish to see in the world, and resistance members are stepping up to be that change every day. As we write these words, we are now marking the one-year anniversary of Trump's election and just recently participated in the second Women's March—Kathy in DC, Donna in Austin. We can confidently and definitively report that it is true: Trump *is* making America great again...just not in the way he anticipated!

Clarissa Pinkola Estés, poet and author of the best-selling book *Women Who Run with the Wolves*, writes, "Do not lose heart. We were made for these times." Are we committed enough to stand up, shout out, and act—one person at a time, one vision at a time?

*Epilogue*

The road ahead may be long and arduous. It will be vital to use every resource and tool at our disposal—especially love. There is no cost or downside to love. Martin Luther King, Jr., Mahatma Gandhi, Jesus, John Lennon, Maya Angelou: they all knew the answer was love. Will we listen?

With love and gratitude,
Donna and Kathy

> *And in the end, the love you take is equal to the love you make.*
> —The Beatles

# Endnotes

Dr. Martin Luther King, Jr., "The Struggle for Racial Justice," Address delivered at the Nobel Peace Prize Recognition Dinner, January 27, 1965. From the papers of Dr. Martin Luther King, Jr., The King Center. http://www.thekingcenter.org

Michael J. Fox, Interview with Dotson Rader, *Parade Magazine*, March 29, 2012. parade.com/40559/dotsonrader/michael-j-fox-excerpt/

Glenn Kessler, "The Fact Checker," *Washington Post*, October 25, 2017

Jeff Malone, in a private Facebook post

Kelley Kosow, *The Integrity Advantage: Step Into Your Truth, Love Your Life, and Claim Your Magnificence*, Sounds True (Boulder, Colorado, 2017), xvi. KelleyKosow.com/the-book/

Madisyn Taylor, "Taking a Time Out," DailyOM online, 2017. Retrieved from http://www.dailyom.com/cgi-bin/display/printerfriendly.cgi?articleid=57255

Brother Thầy Pháp Dung, Buddhist monk, in "Love in Action," a conversation with Jo Confino, executive editor of *The Huffington Post*. http://www.youtube.com/watch?v=xJyJV5p6hvw published Feb 22, 2017

Tori DeAngelis, "When Anger's a Plus," *Monitor on Psychology*, American Psychological Association, March 2003, Vol. 34, No. 3. http://www.apa.org/monitor/mar03/whenanger.aspx

Molly Ball, "Donald Trump and the Politics of Fear," *The Atlantic*, September 2, 2016. Retrieved from http://www.theatlantic.com/politics/archive/2016/09/donald-trump-and-the-politics-of-fear/498116/

Maya Angelou, Interview with Dave Chappelle, aired on The Sundance Channel, May 29, 2014. Retrieved from http://www.youtube.com/watch?v=okc6COsgzoE

Wade Boggs, National Baseball Hall of Fame Induction Ceremony Speech, 2005. Retrieved from http://www.youtube.com/watch?v=8QL141TMrKs

Parker J. Palmer, "Be Not Afraid," LivingLifeFully.com. Retrieved April 2018. http://www.livinglifefully.com/flo/flobebenotafraid.htm

Václav Havel, *The Power of the Powerless* (October 1978). Retrieved from http://hungarianreview.com/article/20170719__the_power_of_the_powerless_and_living_in_truth_in_democracy

Mother Teresa, *In the Heart of the World: Thoughts, Stories, and Prayers* (New World Library, Novato, California, 1997)

Mahatma Gandhi, Letter to Jawaharlal Nehru, in John S. Moolakkattu and Triloki Nath Khoshoo, *Mahatma Gandhi and the Environment: analysing gandhian environmental thought* (The Energy and Resources Institute, New Delhi, 1945)

Pablo Picasso, Statement to Marius de Zayas, in "Picasso Speaks," *The Arts*, New York, May 1923; reprinted in Alfred Barr, *Picasso* (Museum of Modern Art: New York 1946), 270-1. Retrieved from http://www.learn.columbia.edu/monographs/picmon/pdf/art_hum_reading_49.pdf

Arthur C. Evans, president of the American Psychological Association, in a letter to Time magazine, November 1, 2017. Retrieved from http://time.com/5005076/stress-anxiety-symptoms/

*Endnotes*

Audre Lord, *A Burst of Light: Essays* (Firebrand Books: Ithaca, New York, 1988)

Mary McCoy, "What Is Self-Care—Definition, Tips & Ideas for a Healthy Life," MoneyCrashers.com, August 19, 2013. Retrieved from www.Money crashers.com/self-care-definition-tips-ideas/

Thich Nhat Hanh, *At Home in the World* (Parallax Press: Berkeley, California, 2016)

Sgt. Raj Johnson, Interview with Dan Harris, ABC News. http://abcnews.go.com/WNT/video/arizona-police-chief-introduces-officers-meditation-52002004

Gail Stearns, "Self-Care in a Trump Age," *Huffington Post*, February 7, 2017. Retrieved from http://www.huffingtonpost.com/entry/self-care-in-a-trump-age_us_58996b54e4b02bbb1816bf59

"US at 'Lowest Point We Can Remember;' Future of Nation Most Commonly Reported Source of Stress," *Stress in America* Survey, American Psychological Association, November 1, 2017. Retrieved from http://www.apa.org/news/press/releases/2017/11/lowest-point.aspx

Steve Jobs, quoted in Steven Levy, "Steve Jobs, 1955–2011," *Wired*, October 5, 2011. Retrieved from http://www.wired.com/2011/10/steve-jobs-1955-2011/

Diane Altomare, *Clarity: Ten Proven Strategies to Transform Your* Life (Select Books: New York, NY, 2016)

Lynne Twist, in a private Facebook post, March 26, 2017. Retrieved from https://mtouch.facebook.com/story.php?story_fbid=10154842475015617&id=72483805616

155

Dr. Carmen Harra, "A Vision For Your Future," *Huffington Post*, January 2, 2014. Retrieved from https://www.huffingtonpost.com/dr-carmen-harra/future_b_4493573.html

William (Bill) Copeland, quoted in Constance Staley, *Focus on College Success* by Constance Staley, Cengage Learning's Focus Series (Cengage Learning: Boston, MA, 2013)

Prince Charles, in A Royal View, BBC Reith Lecture, 2000, quoted in David G. Myers, "The Perils and Power of Intuition," Psychology Today, November 1, 2002. Retrieved from http://www.psychologytoday.com/articles/200211/the-powers-and-perils-intuition

Robert Wright, "Mindful Resistance Is the Key to Defeating Trump," Vox.com, October 19, 2017. Retrieved from http://www.vox.com/the-big-idea/2017/10/2/16394320/mindful-resistance-key-defeating-trump-mindfulness

Henrik Edberg, "7 Common Habits of Unhappy People," The Positivity Blog, October 5, 2011. Retrieved from https://www.positivityblog.com/7-habits/

Chris Creed, "The Same 24 Hours," Blog post, Oct. 24, 2014. Retrieved from http://chriscreedblog.com/the-same-24-hours/

Bill Keveney, "Sarah Silverman's 'I Love You, America' Seeks Common Ground, with Room for Silliness," *USA Today*, October 20, 2017. Retrieved from https://www.usatoday.com/story/life/tv/2017/10/10/sarah-silverman-i-love-you-america-hulu/740025001/

Steven Stosny, "Chains of Resentment," Psychology Today, September 9, 2011. Retrieved from https://www.psychologytoday.com/us/blog/anger-in-the-age-entitlement/201109/chains-resentment

# Endnotes

Clifford B. Edwards, *The Forgiveness Handbook* (Empower People Ventures: San Diego, CA, 2013)

Anne Lamott, *Traveling Mercies: Some Thoughts on Faith* (Random House: New York, NY, 2000)

David Ingber, "This Yom Kippur, Can We Forgive Trump's Voters?" *Tablet*, September 28, 2017. Retrieved from http://www.tabletmag.com/scroll/246089/this-yom-kippur-can-we-forgive-trumps-voters

Jane Goodall, private Facebook post, July 18, 2016. Retrieved from https://www.facebook.com/janegoodall/posts/10154360658047171

J.P. McEvoy, "Passing the Hot Potato," *The Rotarian*, (Rotary International, Chicago, IL), May 1947.

Jan Sjostrom, "Conservative think tank leader blames contempt for political divides," *Palm Beach Daily News*, February 1, 2017. Retrieved from http://www.palmbeachdailynews.com/news/local/conservative-think-tank-leader-blames-contempt-for-political-divides/ogwY5lIcOWhp0RtOBXBncP/

Clarissa Pinkola Estes, "Do Not Lose Heart, We Were Made for These Times," *Letter to a Young Activist During Troubled Times*, 2001, 2017. Retrieved from http://www.awaken.com/2017/05/do-not-lose-heart-we-were-made-for-these-times/

John Lennon and Paul McCartney, "The End," *Abbey Road* (Apple Records, 1969).

# Additional Resources

**Shadow and Projection**
*The Dark Side of the Light Chasers*, Debbie Ford, 1999, and *The Secret of the Shadow*, Debbie Ford, 2002; www.DebbieFord.com

"Despite his Lies, Donald Trump is a Potent Truth-Teller," *The Guardian*, February 9, 2017; https://www.theguardian.com/commentisfree/2017/feb/09/despite-lies-donald-trump-potent-truth-teller-shakespearean-fool

**Overwhelm**
*Overwhelmed: Work, Love and Play When No One Has The Time*, Brigid Schulte, 2014; www.brigidschulte.com

https://www.heartmath.org/resources/solutions-for-stress/managing-overwhelm-time-pressure/

"Overwhelmed? These 6 Strategies May Help," Blog post, Psych Central, Margarita Tartakovsky, October 16, 2012; https://psychcentral.com/blog/archives/2012/10/16/overwhelmed-these-6-strategies-may-help/

"Does Your Daughter Know its Okay to be Angry?," *Huffington Post*, Soraya Chemaly, June 8, 2017; https://www.huffingtonpost.com/soraya-chemaly/does-your-daughter-know-i_b_10340394.html

### Integrity
*The Right Questions, Ten Essential Questions to Guide You to an Extraordinary Life*, Debbie Ford, 2004

*The Integrity Advantage: Step Into Your Truth, Love Your Life, and Claim Your Magnificence*, Kelley Kosow, 2017; www.kelleykosow.com

### Meditation
Series of 6 videos on meditation by martial arts and qigong expert Tristan Truscott; https://www.youtube.com/watch?v=6W8UoJr2SWQ

Sound Bowl Meditation; https://www.youtube.com/watch?v=Y6QTd-vbu0uI

### Yoga
"30 Days of Yoga with Adrienne Mischler"; https://www.youtube.com/watch?v=oBu-pQG6sTY

### Prayer
"How to Add More Prayer to Your Daily Routine," Bob Hostetler, Guideposts.org, May 25, 2017; https://www.guideposts.org/faith-and-prayer/prayer-stories/pray-effectively/how-to-add-more-prayer-to-your-daily-routine

### Nature
*Sky Above Earth Below, Spiritual Practice in Nature*, John Milton, 2006
Deep Nature Journeys with Bud Wilson; http://deepnaturejourneys.com/

### Mindfulness
Guided Mindfulness Meditation with Jon Kabat-Zinn; https://www.mindfulnesscds.com/

Healthy Mind Healthy Life; https://www.mindful.org
TED talks on self-care; https://www.ted.com/playlists/299/the_importance_of_self_care

# Additional Resources

Mindfulness Meditation with Sound Healing, Jody Theissen and Gail Stearns; https://itunes.apple.com/us/course/mindfulness-meditation-with-sound-healing/id1198270572

"Self-Care in a Trump Age," Gail Stearns, *Huffington Post*, February 7, 2017; http://www.huffingtonpost.com/entry/self-care-in-a-trump-age_us_58996b54e4b02bbb1816bf59 February 7. 2017

"A 69-Year-Old Monk Who Scientists Call the 'World's Happiest Man' Says the Secret to Being Happy Takes Just 15 Minutes a Day" by Alyson Shontell, *Business Insider*, January 27, 2016; http://www.businessinsider.com/how-to-be-happier-according-to-matthieu-ricard-the-worlds-happiest-man-2016-1

## Getting into Action
*The Right Questions: Ten Essential Questions to Guide You to an Extraordinary Life*, Debbie Ford, 2003

https://www.pinterest.com/scrappinmichele/vision-board-samples/ "How to Connect With Your Divine Energy Self in 4 Steps," Gaia.com, March 6, 2014; https://www.gaia.com/article/how-connect-your-divine-self-4-steps

## The Fatal Four
"How to Train Your Monkey Mind," Mingyur Rinpoche, Tibetan Buddhist Master; https://www.youtube.com/watch?v=n6pMbRiSBPs

"How to Stop Comparing Yourself to Others (and Start Empowering Yourself)" Henrik Edberg, The Positivity Blog, September 3, 2014; http://www.positivityblog.com/comparison-trap/

"Stop Making Excuses for Who and Where You Are," Dan Waldschmidt, Success.com, September 9, 2016; https://www.success.com/article/stop-making-excuses-for-who-and-where-you-are

BEYOND RESISTANCE

"Soul Talk: How to Move From Righteousness to Right-Use-Ness," Russell Bishop, *Huffington Post,* May 5, 2012; https://www.huffingtonpost.com/entry/soul-talk_b_1319547.html

"Self-Rightousness: Why Do Some of Us Think Only We Are Right?," Michelle Roya Rad, *Huffington Post,* August 16, 2011; https://www.huffingtonpost.com/entry/self-righteousness_b_870825.html

"Sudden News Is Upsetting," Tzbadmin, TheZenithBusiness.com, September 5, 2017; https://thezenithbusiness.com/sudden-news-is-upsetting/

"Take in the Good," Rick Hanson, http://www.rickhanson.net/take-in-the-good/

## Forgiveness

*The Forgiveness Handbook,* Clifford B. Edwards, 2013; http://theforgivenesshandbook.com/

"I Believe This Belongs to You", Jan Garrett, JD Martin and Ester Nicholson; https://www.youtube.com/watch?v=Sgo9eOo0ecY

Ho'opnonpono: Hawaiian forgiveness process. It is simply repeating the same four statements over and over. You can direct this toward another and especially toward yourself; http://www.laughteronlineuniversity.com/practice-hooponopono-four-simple-steps/

Transform Ill Will, Rick Hanson; http://www.rickhanson.net/transform-ill-will/

"This Grudge," *So-Called Chaos,* Alanis Morissette, 2004; https://www.youtube.com/watch?v=9_3KrVksWJ4

## Dialogue

"Ten Steps to Effective Listening", Dianne Schilling, Forbes,com,

*Additional Resources*

November 9, 2012; https://www.forbes.com/sites/womensmedia/2012/11/09/10-steps-to-effective-listening/#7f256d3f3891

"Bipartisan 'Bromance' Blossoms As 2 Texas Congressmen Make D.C. Road Trip," Jessica Taylor, NPR.com, March 15, 2017

*No Is Not Enough: Resisting Trump's Shock Politics and Winning the World We Need*, Naomi Klein, 2017

*Presence: Human Purpose and the Field of the Future* by Peter M. Senge, C. Otto Scharmer, Joseph Jaworski, and Betty Sue Flowers, 2005

"Practicing Listening Skills," Department of Veterans Affairs, Office of the Dispute Resolution Specialist; http://www.au.af.mil/au/awc/awcgate/va/mediation/listen.htm

"How to See Past Your Own Perspective and Find Truth," Patrick Lynch, Ted Talk; https://www.ted.com/talks/michael_patrick_lynch_how_to_see_past_your_own_perspective_and_find_truth/discussion#t-23945

"17 Tips For a Politically Open Mind," Jean-Pierre Maeli, ThePoliticalInformer.com, August 28, 2015; http://thepoliticalinformer.com/tips-for-a-politically-open-mind/

*Braving the Wilderness: The Quest for True Belonging and the Courage to Stand Alone*, Brené Brown, 2017

# Acknowledgments

We are beyond grateful to friends, old and new, and our families, who encouraged and supported us on this journey.

Tom Parish, who witnessed our process day after day, thank you for the enthusiastic moral and technical support, and all your great ideas along this journey. We are eternally grateful.

Sam Kinter, thank you for your patience each time you had to wait for your mom's attention while we were working.

Richard Hertz, for your generosity of heart and spirit. Your continued desire to learn and make a difference in the world inspires us both.

Liz Meador, thank you for your extraordinary editing support, which went well beyond the call of duty.

Kelley Kosow, you generously provided insight and guidance that helped us find our way through a daunting process. We are forever grateful.

BEYOND RESISTANCE

Arielle Ford, thank you for sharing your expert publishing world wisdom and supporting us on this journey.

Diane Altomare and Krystyna and Tony Clarke, your guidance in navigating the publishing world has been invaluable. Thank you.

Sam, Kendra, Nancy, Justin, Juliet, Lily, Lauren, and Ryan, you are amazing examples of beautiful young people doing good in the world. Thank you for adopting me. Harper, Asher, Siena, Indigo, Oray, Ella, and Luke, I love being your Nana. My deepest desire is to make the world a better place for you. Love, Donna

Adrian East and David and Jana Hart, thank you for keeping Donna in stitches.

Jeff Malone and Mary Herndon, thank you for your love and always holding the light.

Justin Hilton, thank you for providing us a nurturing space for our first retreat. It allowed us to embrace the next level of our writing journey. You have always been there. You are my muse. Love, Donna.

Susan Meredith, thank you for your positive feedback and for being an extra set of eyes!

Terri Weir, thank you for sharing your very special Twitter know-how and getting us off to a strong start!

## Acknowledgments

Alice Peck, Ruth Mullen, Duane Stapp, and the Wasabi Publicity team for your uncompromising commitment to excellence.

Everyone who told us, upon hearing about *Beyond Resistance*, "OMG! I need this book." You kept us going!

A loving thank-you to those who shared their personal stories and to those who took an interest, asking about our progress on the book each time we spoke. You know who you are. ❤

And finally, to Debbie Ford who so generously shared her love and brilliance with us:

Thank you for being my friend and teacher – you have left a loving handprint in my heart. Because I knew you, I have been changed for good. Love, Donna

I am eternally grateful for the gifts you shared with me, they changed my life profoundly. Love, Kathy

# About the Authors

Donna Lipman began her life coaching and presentation skills training career when she was introduced to the work of *New York Times* best-selling author and transformational thought leader Debbie Ford. Reading Ford's books and participating in her Shadow Process workshop set Donna on an eighteen-year journey of personal growth and enabled her to touch the lives of thousands of clients and students.

Donna serves on the Board of Challenge Day, a nonprofit organization designed to support connection and anti-bullying in schools (www.challengeday.org). She is often found in India or Korea, training technology innovators in presentation skills through the University of Texas.

When Donna is not playing with her seven grandchildren, teaching, protesting, contacting her elected officials, or supporting candidates, she is singing with her a cappella group, the Texas Lovebirds. Donna's motto is, "Every voice matters."

She lives in Austin, Texas, with her beloved husband, Tom Parish.

## BEYOND RESISTANCE

Life coach Kathy Hertz proudly describes herself as "a card-carrying member of the resistance." She is the recipient of the George H.W. Bush Points of Light Award for volunteerism and a committed refugee activist. Service has been a major theme running throughout Kathy's life. She believes volunteerism is a form of activism.

Kathy served as a political appointee at the Department of Defense during the Clinton Administration and has worked on numerous political campaigns. Kathy was part of the management teams of David Bowie and Pat Benatar, among others.

Kathy believes it is imperative that we address the epidemic levels of distress and overwhelm following Trump's election if we wish to avoid a public health crisis. She has brought together her coaching and activist experience to create *Beyond Resistance*.

Hailing from New York City, Kathy now lives in a suburb of Washington, DC with her teenage son, Sam, and their three beagles: Charlie, Rocky, and Belle.